W9-AVC-104

Ketogenic Diet
The Step by Step Guide
For Beginners

Jamie Ken Moore

© Copyright 2016 by Jamie Ken Moore - All rights reserved.

This document is geared towards providing exact and reliable information in regards to the topic and issue covered. The publication is sold with the idea that the publisher is not required to render accounting, officially permitted, or otherwise, qualified services. If advice is necessary, legal or professional, a practiced individual in the profession should be ordered.

From a Declaration of Principles which was accepted and approved by a Committee of the American Bar Association and a Committee of Publishers and Associations. In no way is it legal to reproduce, duplicate, or transmit any part of this document in either electronic means or in printed format. Recording of this publication is strictly prohibited and any storage of this document is not allowed unless with written permission from the publisher. All rights reserved.

The information provided herein is stated to be truthful and consistent, in that any liability, in terms of inattention or otherwise, by any usage or abuse of any policies, processes, or directions contained within is the solitary and utter responsibility of the recipient reader. Under no circumstances will any legal responsibility or blame be held against the publisher for any reparation, damages, or monetary loss due to the information herein, either directly or indirectly. Respective authors own all copyrights not held by the publisher.

The information herein is offered for informational purposes solely, and is universal as so. The presentation of the information is without contract or any type of guarantee assurance.

The trademarks that are used are without any consent, and the publication of the trademark is without permission or backing by the trademark owner. All trademarks and brands within this book are for clarifying purposes only and are the owned by the owners themselves, not affiliated with this document.

Table of contents

Introduction

First of all, I would like to congratulate you for taking this step in moving forward on the journey to better health and effective weight loss. I am glad that this guide would be of actionable value to you and thank you for downloading this book, *"Ketogenic Diet. The Step by Step Guide for Beginners: Optimal Path to Effective Weight Loss"*.

Many have tried to do the weight loss regimes of maintaining different diets, adding on the weight loss pills and shakes, then religiously using certain exercise machines bought during the late night browsing of the TV or the web, only to have it either fail in the pursuit of weight loss or to achieve some nominal success but then gain back all the weight and more when the dieting becomes too tough to endure. Does this all sound familiar? .

What would you think if somebody were to tell you that you would be able to lose weight effectively, gain more energy in your daily life and really, really enjoy better overall health if it just needed a change in your diet that doesn't drive you crazy with hunger pangs whilst you are on it?

The ketogenic diet is one diet that is able to fulfil all that and perhaps more with its primary focus on a low carbohydrate intake, moderate protein and high healthy fat dietary content. The diet gives you the ability to lose weight due to fat burning processes that occur the whole day, even in your sleep!

This book will draw up the benefits of the ketogenic diet for you, talk about how and why the ketogenic diet works and most importantly, give you structured easy to follow steps on getting started and maintaining the ketogenic diet for the benefits of weight loss and better health.

I really do hope this book will serve to give you the confidence and knowledge to start embarking on your own personal ketogenic journey. Cheers!

Chapter 1
Ketogenic Diet: The Essentials

What is the Ketogenic Diet?

You all know that our body needs energy for its functioning and the energy sources come from carbohydrates, proteins, and fats. Owing to years of conditioning that a low fat carbohydrate rich diet is essential for good health, we have become used to depending on glucose (from carbohydrates) to get most of the energy that our body needs. Only when the amount of glucose available for energy generation decreases, does our body begin to break down fat for drawing energy to power our cells and organs. This is the express purpose of a ketogenic diet.

The primary aim of a ketogenic diet (called simply as keto diet) is to convert your body into a fat-burning machine. Such a diet is loaded with benefits and is highly recommended by nutritional experts for the following end results:

- Natural appetite control
- Increased mental clarity
- Lowered levels of inflammation in the body
- Improved stability in blood sugar levels
- Elimination or lower risk of heartburn
- Using of natural stored body fat as fuel source
- Weight loss

The effects listed are just some of the numerous effects that take place when a person embarks on a ketogenic diet and makes it a point to stick to it. A ketogenic diet consists of meals with low carbohydrates, moderate proteins, and high-

3

fat content. The mechanism works like this: when we drastically reduce intake of carbohydrates, our body is compelled to convert fat for releasing energy. This process of converting fats instead of carbohydrates to release energy is called ketosis.

A Little History

The ketogenic diet can very well trace its roots to the ancients, where it was purported that the diet was part of the therapy used to treat epilepsy. Hippocratic medicine practitioners, named after the famed physician of the same name, believed in treating the epileptic seizures and the accompanying symptoms of epilepsy using dietetic therapy, where the role of dieting and fasting played a large part in the success of the treatment.

The ketogenic diet was also very much present during the 1920s and 1930s as an effective treatment tool to control seizures in refractory childhood epilepsy. However when the anticonvulsant medication Dilantin surfaced in 1937, the masses were swift to embrace the quick but temporary solution found in the drug and discarded the natural means of therapy.

As luck would have it, the ketogenic diet has seen something of a renaissance in recent times, which coincided with the fact that researchers were starting to finally agree that not all fat was bad, and that mostly it was good fat that is present in most natural food sources.

This wouldn't be a surprise as the keto diet emphasizes a lot on natural dietary fat consumption. With this resurgence of a natural dietary option that changes the way your body fuels itself, I am glad to be amongst the people who have benefited from this diet. You will too, just read on!

Ketosis Need to Know

Ketosis is essentially a metabolic state that draws its name from ketones that are produced when the body switches from using carbohydrates to burning fats as a primary means to power the body's organs and cells. Ketones have been found to be the preferred fuel source for the majority of our body organs, especially the heart as well as the brain, and it is essentially the state of ketosis which brings forth much of the benefits you will experience.

Yet there have been some quarters which voice negativity over ketosis, which sounds similar to the word ketoacidosis, the latter being a life threatening situation that develops in type 1 diabetics. Doctors are worried about ketoacidosis because it occurs when type 1 diabetics cannot produce enough insulin, which then leads the body to think that there is no glucose available and hence burn fat, which produces the much underrated ketones for energy.

The problem here lies in the fact that the type 1 diabetics typically still have high levels of glucose in their blood even as they are producing ketones. The glucose simply cannot be utilized by the body because of the lack of insulin, which acts as a guide so to speak, for the glucose to enter our cells. This leads to a dangerous build-up of high blood sugar and ketone levels which can potentially induce coma and be definitively life threatening.

However, it has to be firmly stated at this point that it is virtually impossible for this to happen in non-diabetics as there will be proper insulin production to regulate blood sugar levels. Also, ketoacidosis is dangerous because of the presence of both heightened levels of glucose as well as ketones in the blood stream, but when ketosis is utilized for your daily energy needs, blood glucose levels will drop naturally, which makes logical sense as glucose for the most part is derived from carbohydrates and hence with a diet that emphasizes on low levels of intake for carbs, glucose levels will fall in line to the optimal range.

How do Ketogenic Diets Work?

For the most part, when someone talks about this or that diet, it will usually conjure up images of constraint, hunger, calorie counting and the assorted inconveniences that many have to put up with to see any sort of success with the traditional calorie restriction diets.

The fundamental basis of most diets for weight loss inherently involves calorie restriction via carefully calculating the allowed calorie consumption with the express goal of letting the body burn more calories than it takes in on a daily basis. After all, the fats that most people are so eager to get rid of are actually the product of excess calorie intake that usually shows itself as excess glucose in the bloodstream, which is then metabolized by the liver into fatty acids that are then stored in our body's favorite areas of adipose fat cells like the stomach, hips and yes, your chin.

When we restrict calories, we are actually trying to tell our body to burn off those fat cells that have accumulated over the years. But here is the problem, for a body that has been attuned to burning carbohydrates for fuel, even with the plentiful abundance of adipose fat being present, the body just doesn't. It is just like a person going to a buffet without recognizing that it is in fact a buffet!

Ketogenic diets on the other hand, rarely if ever has any calorie restrictions, mainly due to the fact that the diet, when subsisting mostly on healthy dietary fat, is actually incredibly satiating. It is this satiating effect, coupled with the diet's ability to control and keep in check hunger pangs much better than any other diets, that naturally keeps the calorie count in line. Oh, and the juicy bit that your body becomes a fat burner when you are keto-adapted helps too!

Relation between Carbohydrate-based Diets and Hunger

Consumption of carbohydrate diets increases the sugar levels in our blood. Consequently, the pancreatic gland enhances insulin production in order to safely disperse the excessive glucose in your blood stream. Owing to this, you begin to feel hungry again and this process continues resulting in an excessive intake of calories. By restricting intake of carbohydrates, the blood sugar levels are kept under check which, in turn, keeps insulin response action under check and hence the feeling of hunger spikes are avoided.

For any diet to succeed, it has to have the ability to control insulin levels because insulin is the hormone that triggers fat storage in your body. By effectively controlling insulin levels in our bloodstream, we create such an environment in our system that is conducive to limiting fat storage and promoting fat lipolysis, the process that our body uses to breakdown fats stored in our system.

Secondly, ketogenic diets give us the freedom to consume filling and satiating food. Keto diets ensure that you get most of your calories from fats and proteins and foods rich in these two nutrients are both delicious and filling. When you eliminate refined sugars and other carbohydrate-rich foods, you are actually breaking the vicious cycle of feeling hungry through carb consumption and the body's insulin response.

As your body gets keto-adapted and ketosis produces the ketones that power your system, you will find that you may be eating just two or even one large meal a day, and that you hardly feel any hunger. Your body has been adapted to burn fats, be it dietary fat from that avocado half or fats from the adipose tissue around the waist!

Nutritional Requirements of a Ketogenic Diet

In a ketogenic diet, your percentage intake of nutrients should be as follows:

- Fats – 70-75%
- Proteins – 15-20%
- Carbohydrates – remainder 5-15%

To give you an example, based on an average daily calorie requirement of 1800, the macronutrient split of 75% fat, 18% proteins and 7% carbs will yield a nutrient weightage of 150g fat, 81g and 31g of proteins and carbs respectively for your daily intake.

Wait, I see a hand waving frantically at me, how in heavens did I jump from calories to daily macronutrient weightage? The answer would be in the amount of calories that each gram of macronutrient produces. We shall be highlighting this in more detail in the step by step guide, so hang on!

Types of Ketogenic Diets

There are 3 types of ketogenic diets that are practiced. They include:

- Standard ketogenic diet
- Cyclical ketogenic diet
- Targeted ketogenic diet

Standard ketogenic diet – This consists of high-fat, very low-carb, and moderate protein intake. It usually has around 75% fats, 5% carbs, and 20% proteins. A ***high-protein ketogenic diet type*** is also usually included here wherein the nutritional ratio consists of 5% carbs, 35% proteins and 60% fats; that is to say, intake of proteins is a little more than the standard keto diet.

Cyclical ketogenic diet – This kind of ketogenic diet consists of periods of ketogenic days followed by higher-carb days; for instance, 5 ketogenic diet days followed by 2 higher-carb days or it could be a full week of keto diet followed by 1 higher carb day.

Targeted ketogenic diet – This type gives you the freedom to enhance intake of carbohydrates around your workout times.

It is important for you to know that only the standard and the high-protein keto diets are the ones that have been studied, researched, and normally recommended, especially for beginners. The other two methods are more advanced and are usually followed by athletes and bodybuilders.

Chapter 2
Going Keto: What's Good About It For You

Low-carb diets including ketogenic diets have been under a lot of flak for a long time. Many people, unknowingly, were of the belief that high-fat content foods carry the risk of increasing cholesterol in the body.

However, for some time now, there have been multiple studies on ketogenic diets and the results have been very, very promising. Ketogenic diets not only help in reshaping your body into an automatic weight loss machine, they also have the capability to reduce metabolic syndrome related risks.

This chapter is dedicated to giving you some amazing benefits of ketogenic diets so that you find ample inspiration to get started on this wonderful journey that has the power to change your life for the better.

Benefits of Ketogenic Diets for Weight Loss

Enhanced weight loss – Reducing carbs is the most effective way to lose weight. This has been the go-to way since the late 1800s for people to trim and drop pounds. There have been several randomized, controlled clinical trials on the turn of the century that showed people on low-carb diets generally lose more weight than those on a low-fat diet with the calorie intake being the same.

By preventing the accumulation of sugars in the body, ketogenic diets drive down insulin production. This compels our body to use up fat stored all around. Even when you are sleeping, the body will be burning fat for its needs! The fat that is being burned is not just the fat you ate but also stored body fat. This will be a huge help in reducing weight.

However, it is important to unfailingly stick to the ketogenic diet that you started with. Slowly but surely, you will definitely see the positive effects on your weight.

It helps you manage your hunger better – The ability to manage and control your hunger is extremely empowering. Hunger is, perhaps, the worst nightmare for anyone going through a diet. It also is the primary reason for people to give up their attempts halfway. Ketogenic diets, on the other hand, reduce hunger and food cravings as they keep you feeling full and satiated.

Fat is a very satisfying and filling nutrient and ketone bodies reduce appetite so you will feel far less hunger than before. In fact, there are times when you might just forget to eat! This is the most exciting part of a ketogenic diet. You are motivated to continue your efforts as you are not struggling with hunger pangs.

Counting calories is likely not going to be very helpful when your body is screaming out for food. On the ketogenic diet, you will feel less hungry and your improved cognitive function will also allow you to judge better the amount of food your system needs.

It enables effortless maintenance of optimal weight – Imagine your body being keto adapted and it is chugging along as an efficient fat burning machine. The amount of effort that you put in to maintain or reduce your weight in order to hit your optimal range would definitely be reduced just because your body is on the fat burning side this time! It is not busy storing up excess fats that your system doesn't use when there is excess glucose.

Exercising to keep fit becomes that, and not a dreaded task just to burn off fats and calories to keep the inches off. Nutritional ketosis will open this door of letting you lose and maintain your weight effortlessly!

It uses stored body fat as fuel – Yes you heard this before and it won't be the last time you hear this, being keto adapted brings about a state where your body recognizes your body fats as a viable source of energy and proceeds to utilize it, thereby generating the ketone bodies for fuel. However, besides stressing the fact that your body fats are being burned whilst being in ketosis, getting your system to recognize those same fats as fuel also enables you to go on intermittent fasting much easier and quicker.

It is not the purpose of this book to expound the merits of going on intermittent fasting, but to reinforce that with your body's fats as a fuel source, should you wish to go on a fast, it would definitely be much easier and the experience better.

It enables faster and better recovery from exercise – On the route to losing weight, exercise would probably be one of the tools that can help. Now, it stands to reason that if exercise were to be helpful for weight loss and our overall health, wouldn't it be better if we were able to recover from those aching muscles and strains on a faster note than what we were used to?

One of the main known causes for those aches and rawness after a workout is essentially your body's systemic inflammation. That in turn has been linked causally to the presence of free radicals formed due to high amounts of sugar intake. On a low carb high fat ketogenic diet, your body's systemic inflammation will go down as a result of lesser carbs and therefore lower glucose levels

This will not be the end where we talk about inflammation, but it suffices at this juncture to say that a lowered state of inflammation encourages body recovery after exercising and working out, and that is good news for most athletes and majority of the people who are keen on serious weight loss.

It reduces and regulates the levels of insulin – Insulin is needed by our bodies to facilitate the usage of glucose or blood sugar. The insulin acts like a sort of messenger between the glucose and our body's cells, telling the cells to essentially open up and start using glucose as an energy source.

On a higher carb diet, our body would essentially be subjected to spikes of insulin every time our blood sugar levels spike due to the need to process it. That sugar has got to go somewhere!

Nutritional ketosis facilitates the reduction of insulin levels purely because your body has lowered levels of blood sugar through lesser consumption of carbs. The insulin spikes are also taken care of when your body switches over to ketones as the primary source of fuel.

Benefits of Ketogenic Diets for Health

Improved cholesterol markers – Cholesterol markers like triglycerides, HDL otherwise known as the good cholesterol, are known to react positively to the ketogenic diet. The LDL, known generally as the villain of the cholesterol panel, usually goes down in most cases in terms of concentration

13

whilst the LDL particle size, where the small dense sizes belong to the category of culprits that push up heart attack risks, normally increase in size to the larger, fluffy kind.

We must note that in order to get your triglycerides levels down, your HDL numbers up and be on your way to having those larger, fluffy LDL particles swimming in your bloodstream, we should be consuming not only a low carb high fat diet, but we must also note the fats which we are taking in. Saturated fats such as those found in fattier cuts of red meats or monounsaturated fats like those found in olive oil are the ones we should be concentrating on. Avoid any vegetable oils like palm, canola or soybean as much as possible for these contain polyunsaturated fats that are detrimental to health.

Improved blood sugar readings – Again, a direct connection to increased consumption of sugar and carbs, blood sugar readings will show marked improvement when you switch to ketogenic diets. On top of that, the ketones which are brought about by the liver's conversion of fats also help out with chronic inflammation that is caused primarily by years of carb eating.

Ketones increases the response of the NRf2 pathway, which serves as a modulator for many genes involving inflammation and cell function. In general, the genes that encourage inflammation are reduced in response while the ones which serve an anti-inflammatory function are upregulated. This means that being on a ketogenic diet essentially reduces inflammation of the body. Besides aiding in muscular and workout recovery, the lowering of systemic inflammatory agents in the body also is a great help with cardiovascular diseases.

Keto diets help greatly to treat metabolic syndrome – Metabolic syndrome refers to a medical condition that enhances risk to heart diseases and diabetes. The metabolic syndrome is, in reality, a collection of syndromes including:

- High blood pressure
- Abdominal obesity
- Low HDL cholesterol levels
- High triglycerides
- High blood sugar levels

All five of the above symptoms can be managed and kept under check by switching to a ketogenic diet consisting of low carbs, moderate proteins, and high fat. Essentially, to reduce risk of having heart disease, the key is to eat more healthy fats from whole and unprocessed foods!

Ketogenic diets help with Epilepsy – This is returning to the literal roots of the initial usage of the ketogenic diet. Since the time of the ancients, the prescribed treatment for fits, which we now know as epileptic seizures, was to allow the patient to go on a fast or for the patients to not consume sugar or starches. Now we know of course that this route would set the body down the path of being converted to a fat burner and thereby producing ketones, which is the key ingredient for the effective treatment of epilepsy.

Documented usage began from the early 1900s where it was used as a go-to approach for epileptic seizures. You would have gathered from the early parts of this book that this form of treatment progressed well into the 1940s, where the inventions of antiepileptic medicines which offered fast relief of the symptoms, put this natural dietary approach onto the backburner.

Fortunately, the diet rediscovered some of its past popularity when Hollywood made a movie of it and right now, we have a healthy wave of adopters who are enjoying epilepsy free lives without the side effects of medications. This proves that good things do last, yes sometimes they get buried and lost perhaps, but ultimately it will always come back if we look hard enough.

Improving Fatty Liver Disease – Nonalcoholic fatty liver disease usually occurs in individuals who are struggling with obesity. It is potentially life threatening if it is allowed to go untreated and may result in liver failure.

You will need to know this however, the fat that causes fatty liver disease doesn't actually come from any of the saturated or monounsaturated fats that you consume in your diet, but it is derived primarily from carbohydrates. The liver converts these carbohydrates into triglycerides which are then stored back into the liver as fats.

Being on the low carb high fat diet reduces triglyceride levels because of ketosis, where fats in our body and also organs are literally the fuel for our system. With lowered triglycerides, the liver fat does not build up fat but instead regresses. In fact, some of the scarring on the liver due to fatty liver disease, known as fibrosis, have been known to improve.

Ketogenic diets help fight many diseases - Ketogenic diets are known to have the potential to fight diseases such as polycystic ovary syndrome (PCOS), Alzheimer's, depression, traumatic brain injury, stroke and others that plague our present generation. There are many studies conducted by reputable institutions that have shown multiple promising results in this aspect. Cancer has also been one of the diseases which is receiving notice with regards to the ketogenic diet due to the growing research on "starving" cancer cells.

The notion of starving cancer cells is not new, where it was brought up back in 1924 by German scientist Otto Warburg who proposed that the prime cause of cancer was derived from the fermentation of sugar within the body's cells.

The primary notion is to remove the sugar or glucose consumption, replace it with dietary fat and the cancer cells, starved of its usual fuel, will then die. It is this book's hope that more clinical trials and research can be done to further this hypothesis and who knows, we might just have a powerful deterrent for cancer.

Benefits of Ketogenic Diets for Lifestyle

You will be more energized – Ketones are a more reliable and sustaining source of energy and you will feel this energy surging through your body. Chronic fatigue symptoms that you had been experiencing till now will go away and you will feel more energetic when you introduce keto diets into your lifestyle.

Due to the cut in reliance on energy from carbs, your body will be spared the "sugar rush" effect, where you get brief surges of energy followed by periods of fatigue. With ketones as your main energy source, your body will be constantly fueled due to the ever present fat burning process going on, just like a lightbulb that remains lit consistently, without the flickers and intermittent outages.

Your mood is enhanced and there is increased clarity in thought – Both these improvements are credited to ketone bodies that are beneficial in stabilizing and controlling neurotransmitters such as dopamine and serotonin. The stabilization of these neurotransmitters helps you control your moods better and improve the clarity of thought.

Doctors who have tracked many of their patients on keto diets say that they have seen improved cognitive functions as well as reduced anxiety. The patients also tend to have better memory and seem to be able to enjoy and live life with lesser dependency on drugs and medications.

Improved digestion – by shifting to a keto diet and reducing sugar and carb intake, you will experience improved digestion and your gut health will also see significant improvement. This is also associated with reduced sugar and grain consumption. The usual bloating and feelings of indigestion will tend to subside.

Enjoy better sleep – With the adoption of the ketogenic diet, you will be more inclined to enjoy a good night's rest. Many keto adapted practitioners report that after being in ketosis, they are able to sleep throughout the night like a baby, without sleep being interrupted in fits and being started awake. These improvements are linked to reduced glucose intake in the daily diet, which tends to facilitate a lower level of chronic inflammation in the system, and thereby allowing the body to ease itself and remain easily in deeper rest.

Who Can Benefit from the Ketogenic Diet?

The answer to the above question is anyone who wants to get the benefits of such a diet. Anyone wanting to lose and maintain their body weight, anyone wanting to become more energetic and active, anyone who wants to manage difficult medical conditions like diabetes and more can feel free to get started on ketogenic diets.

However, there are some clear contraindications to keto diets. We are concerned with primarily people who have history of kidney, liver or gall bladder malfunction issues. The gall bladder is the store of digestive enzymes manufactured from the liver used to breakdown fat, hence these two organs can be said to be fairly important for someone wanting to start off on the high fat based ketogenic diet. Here are some conditions that definitely preempt a physician's approval before starting off on a keto diet:

- History of pancreatitis
- Impaired liver functioning
- Gall bladder related issues
- Impaired fat digestion
- Gastric bypass surgery
- History of kidney failure
- Pregnancy and lactation

While the previously mentioned above are a few conditions listed where it is encouraged that you see your physician before starting off on a keto diet, please feel free to talk to him or her anyway before embarking on your keto journey if you feel uncomfortable. Professional advice is always a good thing.

At the juncture, I would like to reiterate that ketogenic diets are not to be taken as mere diets but an embedded part of your new lifestyle. The effectiveness and success of ketogenic diets will be felt, experienced, and seen only when you find the discipline and fortitude to take the first step forward.

As you can see, ketogenic diets can help you get a lot of benefits, and it is those benefits which will keep you going when you take up this change in diet. Imagine being able to see the scales report back your loss of weight within a few weeks of being in ketosis, and actually being able to keep it there in the optimal range without fear of rebound. How about visiting your cardiologist after a sustained drive in ketosis and having him take you off medications for high blood pressure and other metabolic issues? These are not far-fetched notions, and can be achieved with commitment.

A good ketogenic diet will help you get your energy from fats, a more sustainable energy source than carbohydrates. So, what are you waiting for? Read on, find some simple and delicious recipes in the coming chapters and start working on getting the benefits of a great ketogenic diet!

Chapter 3
Let's Get Started Step By Step

We have talked about what is the ketogenic diet, its roots and usages and definitely its benefits when one gets into the metabolic state of ketosis. We will now leave the "why should you do it" behind for the time being and get started on "how should you do it".

This chapter serves to detail the step by step process with which you can get started on the ketogenic journey. We will be talking about the initial stages of how you should prepare yourself for the diet, what kind of foods you should be looking out for and what should you be expecting whilst on the diet and when you get into full blast ketosis. This is really the portion where you can use it to take action immediately and bring about the positive changes you are looking for.

Step A: First Things First

The most important thing to do before you start off is to take a moment to run through your mind if you have any outstanding physical ailments or problems, particularly if it were related to the gall bladder or liver. If you do not know, it might be a good idea to visit your physician for a full body check up and let him or her know your intentions regarding taking the keto route. Once he or she has given you the all clear signal, you are free to begin your next steps. One thing to note though, do make sure your doctor already knows what the ketogenic diet is all about before you visit, else you might very well be making a wasted trip! If your doctor doesn't know, switch and find one who does.

Then, what you need to do is to calculate your daily macronutrients requirement with an ideal keto diet that suits your requirement. As a beginner, I would suggest that you start off on the standard ketogenic diet (SKD) consisting of 75% fat, 20% proteins, and 5% carbs.

The following will help you get ready with a customized plan for a successful ketogenic diet:

Find out your ideal body weight – For this, there are various calculators that are easily available wherein if you input your height, gender, and age, it will tell you what your ideal body weight should be. However, you need to know how the mechanics work, so we shall be looking at how to arrive at your ideal weight range using the body mass index (BMI) method.

Calculating your BMI using the metric system goes like this, weight in kilograms divided by height in meters squared. BMI using pounds and inches is pretty much the same, with your weight in pounds divided by height in inches squared, but you need to multiply the result with a conversion factor of 703. So if your weight is about 150 pounds and you have a height of about 5 foot 5 inches (65 inches), your BMI calculation goes like this 150 pounds divided by 65 inches squared, then multiplied by 703 (the conversion factor) to get 24.96.

The ideal range for BMI readings is between 18.5 to 24.9, which is classified as normal or healthy weight. Anything above or below this scale would not be desirable. As you can tell, there is a range for optimal weight, listen to what your body tells you as a good gauge.

Find out your daily calorie requirement – This is important because it is the foundation for the later part on the breakup of macronutrients that you need for your daily diet. Though there are many, and I say many, online calculators which allow you to key your weight height and age to find out your daily calorie needs, over here, it is still the belief that you need to know how to get the numbers, so here we go!

For manual calculation of your daily calorie needs, we shall be using the method called the Mifflin-St Jeor formula. For men, the calculation goes like this

- 10 x weight (Kg) + 6.25 x height (cm) − 5 x age (years) + 5

So for a 30 year old man who weighs 180 pounds (81.6kg) and stands at a height of 6 feet (183cm), his total daily intake should be 1,815 calories. For women, it is calculated below

- 10 x weight (Kg) + 6.25 x height (cm) − 5 x age (years) − 161

Similarly for a 30 year old lady who weighs 160 pounds (72.7kg) and measures 6 feet (183cm), her total daily intake will be 1,560 calories. Now that you know what your daily calorie intake should be, it is time for the fun part, knowing how to calculate your macronutrient breakdown. The fat's in the fire, to say the least!

Find out the breakup of fats, carbs, and proteins to be included in your diet – This will help you understand how you can structure your meals so that you know that your daily dietary requirements are fulfilled correctly. We will need to know how many grams of fats, proteins and carbs that you will need.

Right now you already know how many calories per day you need, what is required now is the way to convert the calories to the macronutrient grams that makes it easier to track how much we are eating. So now, with an example of a 1,800 daily calories intake, when translated on the percentage requirements of the standard ketogenic diet of 75% fats, 20% protein and 5% carbs will give us 1,350 calories for fats, 360 calories for protein and 90 calories for carbohydrates.

The next step will be to divide up these calories by the caloric values that each gram of macronutrient yields. Both protein and carbohydrates gives about 4 calories per gram while fats can provide 9 calories per gram. This says something about using fat as body fuel huh? So based on the example of 1,800 calories per day, the standard ketogenic diet will give a guideline of 150 grams of fat, 90 grams of protein and finally about 23 grams of carbs.

This will give you a good idea of how many grams of macronutrients you need per day based on calories intake. One thing to note is that whilst on a ketogenic diet, you generally do not need to count calories, because like what we have been saying all this while, eating a fat based diet is very satiating and fulfilling. There is none of the hunger pangs that accompanies most weight loss diets nor the urges for food once you get fully keto adapted. The guide here is to eat and listen to your body. Eat when hungry, to the point of fulfilment but not stuffing yourself, and you will find that the calories counting will take care of itself.

I would also like to state that when we are talking about carbs, we are just talking about that, and not net carbs. The concept of net carbs has been popularized where you take the total carbs and subtract the fiber content. Unfortunately, the net carbs idea is probably one of the main culprits why many think they are on the ketogenic diet yet fail to enjoy the benefits of nutritional ketosis. So treat carbs as carbs, and limit them to your daily macronutrient guideline.

Items that you may need – At this juncture, we have talked plenty about nutritional ketosis and how it is good for you, but how do you know if you are indeed in a state of nutritional ketosis? This is where we need to talk about how ketones are measured and what are the tools you can use to measure them.

There are three types of ketone bodies that we are interested in

- Acetoacetate – the primary body found in urine
- Beta-hydroxybutyrate – ketone found in blood
- Acetone – the ketone body found in our breath

Due to cost and ease of use, testing for ketones found in the urine has been one of the more common ways to see if you are on your way to ketosis. However, testing via urine is largely imprecise. This is because the urine strips that are used to measure ketones are largely meant for diabetics who are testing for ketoacidosis, hence the strips are programmed to pick up larger doses of ketones. Also, as your body transits from burning sugar to fat, ketones are produced in larger amounts, hence when you first test for it via urine, it will be positive. However as your body starts absorbing the ketones for energy, moving into ketosis, less of it will be expelled via the urine. So there is a distinct possibility that as your body gets into nutritional ketosis, you wouldn't even know as the urine strips turn up negative results! Don't do this to your-self, it is very disheartening.

The other, more accurate way of testing for ketones would be via blood testing. This way is usually done via a prick of your finger for the blood to be dapped on the test strips for analy-sis using the blood ketone monitors. Ketosis is shown to be present when our blood ketone levels are around 1 to 3 mil-limolar per liter, with some measures going higher to 4 mil-limolar, so testing for ketosis using your blood is indeed the current most accurate way. However, the disposable strips used for testing are quite expensive, not to mention the mat-ter of pricking yourself daily to check for blood ketone levels. I'm one such person who don't really fancy the pain, espe-cially on a daily basis!

So what then for those who don't want blood testing? Fortu-nately, there is the option of breath testing, which measures the amount of acetone present in your breath using a breath monitor. Essentially you breathe or exhale for about 10 to 15 seconds to force out the air that is at the bottom of your lungs into the monitor. Breath ketone bodies have been found to be as reliably correlated as blood ketone bodies to nutritional ketosis. Personally I am testing for ketosis using the Ketonix breath ketone monitor, since it just needs a hard blow and there is no pain. More importantly, the results are the same as blood ketone testing. At this point, I would like to bring a word in about testing for ketones using the police breathalyzers, where there has been some talk about it. I can only say, use the right tool for the uses it is meant to do, and considering the breathalyzers are about a third more expen-sive than ketonix, I reckon it better to just stick to that.

Prep it slow or take the plunge – This segment will touch on how you want to begin your ketogenic journey. Remember we are essentially switching from being sugar burners to being fat burners when we phase into ketosis. This transition is not without its slight share of troubles. Imagine your body having gorged itself on glucose from all the carbs that you have been consuming for the past twenty or thirty years, and now all of a sudden, your body is going to be severely deprived of the glucose buffet, the consequence is very much like a addiction withdrawal.

There is basically two ways to go about the transition. One, you take a deep breath and jump into the deep end, restricting your carb intake to that 20 or 30 grams on a daily basis. Two, you go slow on your body, and ease into the carb restriction over a period of a week or two, but no longer than that. You start by setting a conscious limit of how many grams of carbohydrates you will be consuming, perhaps 100 to 150 grams, and then cutting down 10 grams every day. This way your body gets used to lower carb intake gradually.

It is a personal choice on which route you wish to take when you start off pursuing ketosis. For me though, it has always been an all or nothing mentality, so I did the cold plunge right in. Boy, was the water in the deep end cold! The good thing about it was that it was pretty easy to stick to the low carb intake after the initial 1 or 2 days, but like I said earlier, this portion is up to personal choice and comfort.

Step B: Getting Your Pantry Ready

This is the part where you actually target the various food items which will be part of the ketogenic diet, though by no means exhaustive, it should serve as a rough guide on what should be eaten and what is to be avoided. At the very beginning, clear your kitchen out and make sure that no food high in carbs is even available close at hand. This includes most chocolates, candy, bread, sugary drinks, pasta, and rice. Do a complete carb sweep of your pantry! Restock your kitchen with the following keto items.

Meats and animal products – Please avoid farmed animal meats and processed meats like sausages, hot dogs, and meat that come in starch or sugary starches.

- Grass-fed meat including venison, lamb, beef, chicken, pheasant, sheep, rabbit, and goat
- Wild-caught fish including anchovies, cod, eel, mackerel, tuna, trout etc.
- Seafood caught in the wild including abalone, caviar, crab, clams, mussels, scallops etc.
- Pastured poultry and pork
- Pastured eggs
- Ghee
- Gelatin
- Butter
- Offal from grass-fed animals; kidney, heart, liver, bone marrow, tripe, tongue and other organ meats

Fats – Take in more saturated and the monounsaturated variety.

- Saturated fats including tallow, lard, duck fat, chicken fat, goose fat, clarified butter (ghee), coconut oil, butter etc.
- Monounsaturated fats like avocado oil, macadamia oil, and olive oil

- Fats rich in polyunsaturated omega-3s extracted from animal sources
- Coconut butter, cocoa butter
- Dark Chocolate (90% or higher)
- Chia Seeds
- Palm shortening

Vegetables – Avoid root vegetables and stick to green leafy ones so as to keep your carb intake low. You can include fermented vegetables like kimchi and sauerkraut

Artichokes	Asparagus
Bell peppers	Broccoli
Cabbage	Carrots
Cauliflower	Celery
Cucumber	Chives
Aubergine (eggplant)	Fennel
Garlic	Kohlrabi
All leafy greens	Lettuce
All kinds of mushrooms	Onions
Okra	Radishes
Pumpkin	Scallion
Spinach	Tomatoes
Watercress	Zucchini
Shallots	
All kinds of seaweeds	

Fruits – Most fruits are off the list of keto diets due to the high levels of fructose. However, very small amounts of berries are allowed; yet it is important to watch which fruit and how much you consume.

Avocado	Blackberry
Olive	Lemon and Lime

- Blueberry   Strawberry
- Raspberry   Cranberry

Legumes – Like fruits, almost all kinds of legumes off limits in keto diets, but small amounts of peas and green beans can be included in your meals.

Dairy products – For the initial month of your foray into ketogenic diets, keep dairy products out for those who don't know if they can tolerate dairy. Then reintroduce them slowly and watch for any adverse reaction before including them in your meals. Full-fat dairy, unpasteurized, and raw dairy suits best.

- Kefir and Full-fat yogurt
- Full-fat raw cheeses
- Ghee and Butter
- Full-fat sour cream
- Heavy Whipping Cream
- Full-fat cottage cheese
- Full-fat cream cheese

Drinks – All aerated and sweetened drinks will have to be completely and unequivocally avoided. And keep a look out for hidden sugars in your drink. Definitely, include plenty of water. The following drinks are good for ketogenic diets:

- Coconut milk   Almond milk
- Cashew milk   Herbal teas
- Broth and soups   Water
- Coffee and tea   Seltzer water
- Lemon and lime juices   Club Soda
- Sparkling mineral water

Nuts and seeds – While nuts and seeds are very delicious, it is easy to get carried away and end up eating more than you should. So, be wary of nuts and keep them under control. Moreover, nuts and seeds enhance your carbohydrate intake, so it is all the more important to be cautious. An important note to remember is peanuts are legumes and hence are to be avoided. You can include the following in your meals:

• Almonds	Hazelnuts
• Macadamias	Pecans
• Psyllium seeds	Pistachios
• Pine nuts	Sesame seeds
• Pumpkin seeds	Cashew nuts
• Sunflower seeds	Walnuts
• Butters made from various nuts	
• Chia seeds	

Herbs and spices – Feel free to experiment with all herbs and spices as they will add a deliciously new dimension to your food. Spices that add amazing flavor and aroma to your food include:

• Black Pepper	White pepper
• Sea salt	Italian seasoning
• Basil	Chili powder
• Garam-masala	Oregano
• Curry powder	Cayenne powder
• Thyme	Turmeric
• Cumin powder	Sage
• Rosemary	Parsley
• Cilantro	Cinnamon
• Nutmeg	Cardamom
• Ginger	Cloves
• Paprika	

Prepping the pantry in a family – For those who are staying alone, revamping your pantry will be easy, just follow the steps to clear away those foods which are high in carbs or donate them away. However, for those who are staying in a family who are not following the ketogenic diet like yourself, prepping the pantry will be a slightly different ball game.

Right off, it would be a vastly easier job if you could separate the pantry space into two portion, one for keto foods and the other for the rest of the folks. Space delineation is a good visual way to help you identify things in a flash and is also very helpful for creatures of habit like ourselves. Next it would be good to keep about a week's worth of food stocked so that it doesn't run the risk of getting stale or past its expiry date.

It would also be good if your family members can sort of buy in to the idea of you getting started on the ketogenic diet, so that there wouldn't be any undue pressure on you during your journey. Things like "Are you crazy! Those are fats!" and "I've heard things about this diet, and it causes heart failure" kind of statements, while well-meaning are unfortunately misplaced. Once they get pass this initial stage of concern, when they start seeing the benefits of ketosis surfacing for you, weight loss, healthier cholesterol count, increased energy among many others, then they might also hop on the bandwagon!

Key foods that your diet will depend on – This portion here will be covering the various foods which will be relied on to achieve ketosis and fulfil your macro as well as micronutrient requirements as much as possible. Think of this as a sort of a mini primer list, where the foods listed are suitable for the ketogenic diet due to their specific macro and micronutrient content.

• Strawberry - Though in our fruit section earlier on, there was mention of other berries like blue or blackberries which are suitable for the keto diet, strawberries are much better bang for the buck. Compare the 14 grams of carbs present for blackberries against 8 grams for strawberries in every 100 grams of the fruit, strawberries definitely allows for more consumption under the low carb diet. They also supply iodine as well as vitamin C, essential for our body's thyroid optimal function.

• Coconut oil – This oil will be able to boost ketone production if one were unable to enter ketosis when following the ketogenic diet. It has the same effects as the medium chain triglycerides (MCT) oils in that the medium chain fats can be readily broken down into ketones. In addition to helping the body achieve ketosis, coconut oil is also massively known for its anti-inflammatory effects.

• Olive oil – This is the oil that is very much touted to be healthy and essentially an agent for arresting or suppressing cardiovascular diseases. You could probably use this oil very liberally, either when cooking or as a condiment, if you are facing fairly strong resistance from your friends and family on your fat consumption. They probably would be nodding approvingly about your use of olive oil. 1 tablespoon contains 15ml or grams of oil, of which 3 grams are saturated fat, whereas the rest would be monounsaturated fat. Olive oil also contains vitamins E and K as well as biologically active antioxidants. On top of that, it is rather tasty too! For me, I use it as a quick charge of fats for my daily diet, especially if I am on the move a lot that day. It is also an alternative to coconut oil if, like some of my friends, you really do not like the smell of coconut oil. For the rest who do, then you have the luxury of getting the best of both worlds by satiating yourself on both of the oils.

• Whole eggs – One large egg weighs in at about 50 grams, of which 5 grams consist of fat, and proteins take up about 6 grams. It is also an excellent source of selenium, potassium, magnesium and phosphorus. Eating eggs will replenish selenium, which tends to get depleted during the ketogenic journey. Remember, do eat the whole egg, not just the egg whites. Embrace the fact that the keto diet is a fat rich diet, and just consume the whole egg! To put it simply, a chicken would have been grown from the egg, which means the egg must be containing lots of good stuff!

• Cheddar cheese – This will be one of the keto snacks that will come in handy whenever you feel the urge for munching on some food. For those who just started on the keto diet, it will be inevitable that there will be some cravings for the sugary, starchy food or snacks that we are used to. Cheddar cheese or other forms of cheese will be a good fix to that. One slice of cheese weighing 21 grams contains about 5.6 grams of fat and 3.6 grams of protein, throw in the sodium and calcium contained and it will quickly become one of your favorite snacks!

- Macadamia nuts – Nuts as mentioned earlier tend to have a higher carb to fat ratio than most other foods, and because nuts being nuts, there is also that tendency to overeat on nuts just because it is so easy to keep popping them in your mouth and thereby overshooting your carb daily limit. However out of the various nuts, I would go with macadamias as they clock in at a staggering 76 grams of fat, mostly of the monounsaturated nature, whilst the carbs are kept fairly low at 14 grams based on a 100 grams intake of nuts. To help with the measure, 100 grams of nuts works out to be about half to two thirds of a normal cup. Macadamias are also a good source of potassium as well as various essential vitamins. Get the organic non roasted ones for best effect!

- Pastured butter – This will be important because, at the risk of constant repetition, the ketogenic diet will be a fat rich diet, so butters will be a cornerstone of the diet. Pastured butter will be recommended over butters from grain fed cows. Why so? Pastured butter contains more vitamin K2, which helps the body decalcify major arteries and essentially preventing the body's calcium from leaching into the arteries and thereby contributing to heart disease. Butter also has a potent anti-inflammatory agent butyrate that significantly reduces chronic inflammation in our body system. That also helps with reducing cardiovascular disease risk. Imagine this, eating butter actually reduces the risk of heart attack! For those who do not have a dairy friendly gut, try to consume bit by bit to see the effect, say 10 to 20 grams daily. If it does not sit well still, well there is always olive oil to act as a potent secondary cover.

• Dark chocolate – Chocolate! This is of the dark variety, so the cocoa content will be high. In fact, for the diet, it is recommended that we take in at least 90 to 99% dark chocolate, so none of those 50 to 60% stuff, at least at the beginning when you are trying to get into ketosis. Dark chocolate is again one of those healthy foods that is loaded with antioxidants and saturated fat. A 100 gram bar of dark chocolate contains about 51 grams of fat, with which 31 grams are of the saturated variety, while only packing a measly 8 grams of carbs. Dark chocolate is a good food filler for those times when you may feel hungry, just snap off a couple of squares, which usually comes to about 10 grams and you will be fulfilling part of your daily fat requirement!

• Raw walnut butter – While some may swear by raw almond butter instead of walnut, the walnut variety took this place purely because of the presence of its richer omega-3 content. Don't get me wrong, both walnut and almond butters are good food items which can be useful in your keto pantry due to their high fat to carb ratio. 2 tablespoons of butter, approximately 30 grams, will give about 19 grams of fat while clocking up about 1 gram of carb and 6 grams of protein. The great thing about this is you can literally munch on this alone if you are seriously in a rush.

• Pork belly – We are moving into the "meat" of things, pun intended. Pork bellies as well as various fatty cuts of pork and red meats will become one of the staples of your ketogenic diet. Pork belly contains both saturated as well as monounsaturated fat, as well as a lower level of polyunsaturated fat. A 100 gram cut of pork belly will yield 51 grams of fat, of which 19 grams are saturated, 25 are monounsaturated and about 6 grams are polyunsaturated. Its protein content is also fairly low at 9 grams and with zero carbs as can be expected with meat, you will not add further carbs into your diet. At this point, it may still require a bit to wrap your head around eating fats, but as various studies have shown, healthy dietary fat consumption has little correlation to the presence of metabolic syndrome in our body. Do ensure, however that the fats you consume are of the saturated or monounsaturated variety, while if there are polyunsaturated fats present, they are generally coming from whole foods and not manufactured like those we find in the much purported "healthy" vegetable oils.

•   Cauliflower – Wait a minute, what's a distinctively non fatty food item doing on this list? Yup you got me right, this is not a wrong entry. Cauliflower, and the other green leafy vegetables are going to be an essential part of the ketogenic diet. While they are not a major source of fat, they are a large contributory source of the fiber that we need on a daily basis. Broccoli gets in on the list because one of the concerns people tend to have with the keto diets is that the practitioners do not get enough vitamin C and hence develop scurvy. It is not the intent of the book to debate if the keto diet does really cause scurvy due to the lack of vitamin C, but to address how you may be able to find keto friendly sources of vitamin C, now that slurping down that large glass of orange juice, together with all that fructose, is probably out of the question. Cauliflower is one of those ready answers, able to be eaten raw, blended into a paste or lightly cooked, it is one of those versatile veggies that would serve you well. On top of containing quite a bit of vitamin C, it also has not too shabby amounts of potassium which is also an essential nutrient, all the while packing just 5 grams of carbs on 100 grams of cauliflower. I'd say you probably can binge on this and still stay safe within your carb limit! Okay, that was just a kind of exaggeration, it is always not good to binge, but hey, you get the idea about cauliflower. Gives you your vitamin C load ups without an extreme cost on your carb intake.

•   Coconut water – Right, we are back to this round hardy fruit again. We have talked about the oil, and now we shall be touching on the water. Coconut water has one of the most abundant content of electrolytes found naturally. Whilst on the ketogenic diet, we may forget to consume an adequate amount of water and also take care of our electrolyte levels, hence the recommendation of some coconut water once every two days or even daily if it is right up your alley will serve to tip those unbalanced scales of your electrolytes back into balance again. Oh by the way, 100 grams or ml of this water only yields about 5 grams of carbs. You can stagger the way you drink it, perhaps once every two or three days if you are just starting out, then perhaps a little more frequent when you have a firm grasp of your daily carb limit.

•   Button or Shitake mushrooms – These are especially good for replenishing your stores of selenium as well as bulking up on the potassium levels. Mushrooms definitely are not the go-to source of fats, those belong to the dairy and meat produce, but they complement the keto diet in ensuring we have our levels of essential micronutrients taken care of. Besides they are great to cook with!

•   Avocado – This is also one of the more common ingredient fruit which you will find in most ketogenic diets. The avocado fruit is not only high in natural fat content, it also has good levels of potassium and vitamins like C and K, all packed with just 9 grams of carbs for every 100 grams of the fruit. The thing about this is not only just its dense nutrient content, but also just how ridiculously easy it is to prepare and consume this super fruit. Cut and eat it on its own, prep it as a part of a salad bowl or whip it up as a smoothie, it's all good! This is unequivocally one of the mainstay building blocks of the keto diet.

Step C: What to Expect When You Start Ketogenic

Now that we have covered the portion on what to do before embarking on the ketogenic diet as well as touching on the various ingredients essential to the diet, we are now set to explore and fill you in on what to expect when you heave anchor and set sail out of the harbor on your keto journey

You know ketogenic diets are a great way to lose and maintain body weight and the change in lifestyle are full of great benefits (already discussed in the previous earlier chapters). If followed consistently and correctly, keto diets make your body break down fats to ketones, which will be used as energy fuels.

While on a keto diet, your body will undergo a few biological adaptations and/or changes, which will result in the outcrop of a few symptoms. These symptoms usually disappear when your body is keto-adapted. The idea for this particular step is such that with the fore knowledge of what could be happening to your body as you go in ketosis, it would be able to allow you to maintain the diet with a peace of mind. After all, they do say knowledge is power. So without much ado, here are some common signs that you are on the way to becoming ketotic.

Bad breath – Many people on keto diets report bad breath or they report a fruity smell in their breath. This is an effect of enhanced levels of ketones in the body. The acetone present in your breath is the main cause of this. Although unpleasant, this breath is a sure shot sign that you are well on your way to achieving ketosis. A lot of people brush their teeth more frequently or use mint leaves to try and hide the effect of this "fruity" breath.

The great thing about this symptom is that it goes away after being on the keto diet for some time and it is definitely not a permanent fixture. To reiterate, the ketones are expelled through various ways from your body and your breath is one such method too which results in the fruity odor.

Another potential bad breath situation could also be due to prodigious consumption of meats. When we take in too much protein, the resultant ammonia production shoots up and hence bad breath can also happen. Hence for practitioners of the keto diet, we shall have to watch protein intake as much as we need to look out for carbs. Always figure out your macronutrient needs first as illustrated in Step A to get your protein, carb and fat numbers.

Muscle cramps – This is definitely something which is likely to happen when you first start out on the diet, especially if you are already packing on quite a fair bit of excess pounds. The cramps are usually caused by an imbalance in our electrolyte levels, as well as a typical drop in sodium and fluid levels when the ketogenic diet is first introduced. Why this happens is because when we start off on the diet, the focus will be very much on fats and to a certain extent protein.

The carb restriction will tend to lead the body to use up its stores of salt, especially if you enforce a very low carb limit like ten or twenty grams per day. The electrolyte imbalance happens due to the fact that you are now faced with a diet change, and consequently may have forgotten to maintain some of the nutrients required. This is why there is that portion in Step B, to ensure optimal levels for both macro and micronutrient intake

Quick fixes on this revolve around three things. Get in more potassium and magnesium, recover your sodium levels and ensure proper hydration. Potassium can be found in abundance through intakes of avocado while dark chocolate provides much of the magnesium needs Also, getting in some coconut water at this juncture may not be a bad thing as well, seeing as it is essentially chockful of essential electrolytes. Drinking bone broths made from pork ribs or beef can fix both the sodium and hydration levels

Finally getting more water into the system is always a good thing to alleviate these muscle cramps.

Feeling of tiredness (short term only) – This symptom is a very common and unpleasant one for first-time keto dieters. The sense of fatigue makes people feeling disillusioned and they stop midway before the body gets a chance to get into a complete ketosis mode. Such people are unable to reap the immense benefits of ketogenic diets.

Let me explain this short-term fatigue to you. You must know that switching from glucose to ketones as energy fuel takes some time and cannot happen overnight. So, initially, you are reducing carb intake and glucose is not sufficiently available for the body. Simultaneously, your body's ability to break down fat molecules for energy is still being built up and has not yet reached optimum levels.

This shortage of energy is what results in the sense of fatigue. Do not give in to the temptation of increasing carb intake. Usually this will hit more frequently for people who just jump straight into the diet itself. Hang in there and perhaps just give yourself a break! Take this opportunity to rest when your body calls for it. Once ketosis sets in (it can take anything from a few days to a couple of weeks depending on your body condition), this sense of fatigue will go away and you will feel more energized than before.

Keto flu – This is some discomfort that can extend from a myriad of symptoms which may include feelings of light-headedness, constipation, headaches, diarrhea as well as carb cravings. This collectively is known as the keto flu, which is known to afflict some people who start off on the ketogenic diet. This could also have been the single most important reason why people claim that the diet does not work for them, seeing as that they experience negative effects once the diet commenced.

The thing to note here is that it is part and parcel of the transition from letting your body burn sugar to asking it to burn fat. In effect, it has been probably a while since your body has any need to metabolize fat for energy, since glucose presumably has been readily available most of the time, so the process will be somewhat like stopping a freight train going at fifty miles an hour, you cannot just slam the brakes and expect it to come stock still and immediately reverse direction.

The metabolic train has got to gradually decrease its speed, finally stop, and then start moving in the positive direction. How fast it does that would depend on the state of your rails, which is an allusion to how badly metabolically damaged your body is. Some of the things which may help alleviate the symptoms are to get in more fiber in the form of broccoli and spinach for the constipation. Taking on some more coconut oil can also be helpful. The diarrhea could potentially dive off once you take on some probiotics.

Typically, these symptoms last no more than a few weeks, with some people not getting them at all, and others just coming out of it after a few days. If you do find yourself consistently feeling like this, it may be a signal that your body is failing to get into ketosis.

At this juncture, we would have to go back to the basics and start looking at the amount of carbs and proteins as well as fats you are consuming. Chances are that there has been an over consumption of carbs or under consumption of fats or both. Once we get them sorted out, these feelings of discomfort should go off and it is time to kick back and enjoy the benefits of being in constant ketosis.

Frequent urination in the middle of the night – This is a direct response to the fact that your insulin levels are actually dropping because there is actually lesser glucose intake in your diet. This prompts the kidneys to begin flushing excess fluids from the body and hence frequent trips to the bathroom might be a common feature during the first few days of being in ketosis.

There is also this thing about you potentially taking in more water during this initial period for reduction of those muscle cramps and this could also spur increased visits to the bathroom as well. In any case, this is only temporary and once your body adjusts to the diet and has reached a new balance in its fluid levels, the bathroom visits at night will stop.

Weight loss – I am sure no one is going to complain about this symptom. There are high chances of you showing symptoms of weight loss both in the short term and in the long term. In the first week itself, you might begin to lose weight, and this is due to water loss from the body and the usage of stored carbs.

Water loss is not something which you need to worry about. It is a natural process where the glycogen which was stored in the body is being used up and not replaced due to the low carb diet. Glycogen is comprised mainly of water, hence when it is burned off, water weight in the body system also goes down as well.

The reduced insulin levels also play some part in expelling water weight. With a reduced insulin level, the kidneys are no longer prodded to store more salt and water and hence expel it from the body. This will also contribute to more frequent visits to the toilet until the body gets attuned to a lower insulin level.

However, while significant water weight loss can be experienced in the first or second week of following the keto diet, especially for the more obese or overweight, the more enduring weight loss will come in later when fat burning kicks in. The weight loss should slow down to a more gradual pace until it plateaus at your optimal weight.

This is where you see the benefits of the ketogenic diet for weight loss and optimal weight maintenance in the longer term. As long as you fuel the virtuous cycle of eating sufficient dietary fats to instigate the body into fat burning consistently, you shall be enjoying the fruits of having a body that actually helps you keep the fats off!

Increased levels of ketones in urine – At the start of the ketogenic diet, the first few signs of doing it right generally will be found in the urine, where more and more ketones will be present as the body transits from glucose to fat burning. During this initial stage, many keto diet practitioners get their kicks by testing their urine using the urine strips. Having the strips turn purple gives a visual affirmation that what they are doing is right.

However, this is only for the initial stages, as the ketones in the urine may fade off once the body enters full blown ketosis. This is where the body is attuned to running on ketones for its energy needs, and lesser of it is being "wasted" and expelled via urine. At the latter stages, it would be good and useful to switch over to breath-testing for affirmation that your body has entered and is maintaining the state of ketosis.

You will feel less hungry – This is another common symptom reported by followers of ketogenic diets. You may recall that this is one of the benefits mentioned in the earlier chapters. Having this occur will help you be more attuned to what your body needs and lets you eat while you are truly hungry and not due to hunger caused by insulin spikes.

This is a situation where the norm of having three meals a day literally goes out of the window. Due to the satiating nature of dietary fat, you may find yourself having a fairly large meal at the beginning of the day and not feel the pangs of hunger perhaps until dinner time. This also throws a bit of a problem with regards to social eating, where outings with the folks would invariably lead to food of some kind. At this juncture, it would be good to remember to eat only if truly hungry. Just tell your hosts or friends that you are not hungry or get by with a glass of warm water. If food is really shoved right in front of you and you really have to eat, take a small piece!

Changes in cholesterol markers – In most cases, cholesterol markers will change positively over the medium term, triglycerides will go down due to lower carb consumption, HDL levels will go up while the LDL levels will come down.

However, in the short term, perhaps over one or two weeks from the start of the diet, there may be about a third of the total number of practitioners who may see increased levels of LDL and total cholesterol. This may look intensely alarming but it could be due to the weight loss and fat burning process at the initial stages as the body adjusts to being a fat burner. If there are signs of non-alcoholic fatty liver disease present before the start of the diet, then the increased cholesterol levels initially could also be attributed to the retardation of the fatty liver disease.

The key to this issue is to allow your weight to stabilize and plateau first before taking any cholesterol readings. The reason is that the rapid weight loss could mess about with your lipid panel markers and cause unnecessary panic and worry. If however the total cholesterol as well as the LDL markers still remain elevated even after the wait out period to account for weight plateauing, then it might be prudent to run tests for an underactive thyroid.

If thyroid hormones are low, it affects the body's ability to breakdown and remove the unwanted cholesterol it does not want. Remember, do run a check on the thyroid levels if the cholesterol markers persistently remains high on the wrong side, the keto diet may have just uncovered a case of subclinical hypothyroidism.

While we are not here to discuss how to address the issues of hypothyroidism, I would like to point out that it is a condition that can be reversed by simple changes to the diet and it does not always necessarily need medications. Increasing foods that are richer in iodine and selenium will do wonders to help out with this.

Mushrooms, as pointed out earlier, are great for selenium whilst seaweed like kelp or wakame are equally rich as sources of iodine. More importantly, this does not mean you have to give up your ketogenic diet, especially since the foods which help with the thyroid are also on the list for the keto diet. The benefits of being in ketosis are awaiting, you just need that commitment and discipline to tread the path of going ketogenic!

Step D: What to Look Out For During The Ketogenic Journey

Once you have achieved ketosis, then all that you need to do is continue to remain in ketosis. Firstly, the good things! All those unpleasant symptoms will go away and you will feel more energized and full of mental and physical vigor. You will feel like you are reborn with new a body and new body parts. Okay, that's a trifle exaggerated but you get the drift.

However, for the folks who have gone on the ketogenic diet but have yet to experience the profound benefits of ketosis, this segment is included so that you would be able to check and fine tune on certain aspects in order to cross that threshold and enter into constant nutritional ketosis. Below are the pointers to help keep you in ketosis as well as to possibly give you that extra push if you are not there yet.

Watch your protein intake – The standard ketogenic diet calls for approximately 75% fats, 5% carbs and about 20% protein intake. The thing to watch here is to ensure that we do not overconsume the amount of protein on a daily basis.

Because the diet calls for carbohydrate restriction, it is very easy for people to remember it as such and then associate it with other standard low carb diets, in which many of the said low carb diets would replace carbs with proteins, thus making it a low carb high protein diet. This will be totally detrimental to what you are trying to achieve, which is nutritional ketosis.

When your body has a protein intake that is in excess, what happens is the process called gluconeogenesis, where proteins are converted into glucose by the liver. This is the body's natural way of creating glucose when there is a lack of it through the dietary route, remember we are on low carbs! If there is an excess of protein, gluconeogenesis can also occur, thereby driving up blood glucose levels and insulin production, which then inhibits the production of ketones.

Generally as a rule of thumb, the 20 to 25% of proteins as part of your total calorie requirements would not trigger a situation of excess proteins. However, every individual is different and everyone's protein limit would also be different. If you find you are sticking to the dietary guidelines already and still not seeing ketosis, then it might be time to tweak your protein intake. If 100 grams does not work for you per day, then try dropping 5 to 10 grams and monitor your ketone levels.

Don't avoid or reduce the recommended amount of fat in your meals – Despite getting into ketosis, the deep-seated fear of fat drives people to reduce it below the recommended levels. Don't do this! Fats keep you satiated and full. Remember, fats is the reason why nutritional ketosis kickstarted in your body again after years of carbohydrate and consequently glucose dependency. That is why it is important to stick to the amount that you would have derived from the earlier steps mentioned in this book. Again, at the risk of sounding like a broken recorder, go for saturated fats found in dairy and red meats as well as monounsaturated fats found in olive oil and avocados. Avoid polyunsaturated fats as much as you can. Most importantly, be prepared to eat fat!

Do not starve yourself – Eat your regular meals at the convenient time; however, avoid skipping meals. Skipping meals enhances sugar carvings. Instead, eat the recommended daily portions at frequent intervals keeping track of the total calorie and macros intake. Once you are keto-adapted then there are intermittent fasting options that can help you stay in ketosis better. But that is for later.

Drink sufficient water – This statement is almost a cliché in the language of the follower of any diet. But, the importance of water can never be overstated. It is even more important in low-carb ketogenic diets as your body needs more water to burn fats than to burn glucose. And, it is common for thirst to harass you in the guise of sugar and carb cravings.

Don't go overboard with artificial sweeteners – Artificial sweeteners are, after all, refined foods just like sugar. Just because they do not have an immediate effect on your blood sugar levels does not mean they are ideal and can be consumed limitlessly. There are many reports coming in now wherein people confirm that artificial sweeteners enhance cravings for real sugar! Avoid it as much as possible.

Be wary of emotional hunger – How many times have you reached for cookies and chocolates when you have felt depressed or sad or angry or any such strong emotion? Be careful when you reach for sweets and ask yourself the question, "Why do I want to eat the sweet?" If the answer is based on an emotional status of mind, don't eat the sweet!

Watch your stress levels – Being a scrounged up stress ball can do wonders for your body, not! Stress induces increased levels of cortisol and consequently raises your blood sugar levels and leaves you with hunger pangs. Cortisol, by the way is also produced in copious amounts when you stay up late into the night, seeing as it is our body's way of a fight or flight response. That is the reason why you feel hungry when you stay up late. Take it easy, relax and keep trust in that fact that if you follow the diet, listen to what your body tells you, results will come.

Follow instructions of your diet correctly – If you have chosen a diet that says only 20 grams of carbs, stick to it. Count the number of carbs and stop when you have reached that 20 or whichever number the diet prescribes. You don't try to reinvent a diet plan on your own. Tried and tested methods will go awry! Finally, don't give up on yourself; patience, diligence, and commitment are key elements for the success of anything in your life and so with ketogenic diets. So, now that you know the key factors of what makes a ketogenic diet tick, let us carry on to talk about how ketogenic diet impacts weight loss.

Chapter 4
Ketogenic Diet For Weight Loss

This is going to be an interesting portion that we are moving into. Weight loss! And more importantly how the ketogenic diet will help to achieve that. We shall be having a brief on what exactly brings about weight loss, the more common principles for successful weight loss and also some useful, actionable tips at the end as well.

What Is Weight Loss

Weight loss is basically weight that you lose when your body undergoes a process of what the experts term as caloric deficiency. This can be achieved either by boosting your calories requirement through building of muscle mass whilst keeping your intake constant, or via calories restriction in the form of a diet where your daily calories intake is designed to be lesser than your daily requirement.

When your body finds itself in a state where calories input are lesser than what it needs for daily function, it will seek to get energy from stores of energy within your body. Most of the time these would be from the stores of glucose found in the liver as well as from your muscle. The other major energy store found in our body would be the fats that we carry on our frame. This is where the tricky part comes in. If your body isn't conditioned for burning fats, it will quickly use up the glucose stores and that is when the feeling of hunger will come in to potentially derail you from your weight loss mission.

Some Common Weight Loss Principles to Note

To help with the process of losing the unwelcome weight from your body, here are some of the more common principles which are good to base your weight loss strategies on.

Keep hunger at bay – Many folks start off on dieting to lose their excess weight and attempt to get healthy but quite a number fail and fall by the wayside. In the end, these folks have to resort to medications and drugs in order to suppress the symptoms and conditions that accompany obesity. It is definitely not a pretty sight, and it sometimes is quite depressing to see people consign themselves to such a fate when more efficient and healthier solutions are actually just around the corner.

They may have started off strong and seen results after some time, but invariably, the one thing that always put paid to these efforts would be the feeling of hunger that many of these diets entail. Take a plain caloric restriction diet plan for example, if your daily requirement works out to be about 1,750 calories, just polishing off a bagel for a snack would set you back by 250 calories. That is like one seventh of your total requirement. Imagine eating seven bagels for the whole day, would that be enough?

The trick of course is to get onto a diet and lifestyle change where you are able to feel full and keep the hunger pangs at bay and yet get your body to lose weight. Know of any diet that does just that?

Be sustainable – There are many ways to lose weight, that is for sure. Getting on the latest fad diet, juicing, fasting, going the vegan way. I have to say as a matter of fact that I hold all these methodologies in high esteem and it is my opinion that each one of them has their benefits for the human body.

Fasting for example, is a good way to let the body rebalance itself and to get rid of toxins that have built up over time. One of the side effects of fasting would be loss of body weight. However, you would not expect a person to fast for a lifetime, without any consumption of food. For any method of efficient weight loss, it must be sustainable in practice to allow for continued shedding of the excess pounds and also to prevent the dreaded bounce back in weight that has plagued so many

One of the benchmarks of sustainability for diets would be the ease of implementing it in everyday life. Imagine if you are on a diet that requires you to eat six to seven small meals a day, you would definitely have to pack for those meals and also find the time to consume them during the work day.

Exercise – Regarded as one of the main pillars for weight loss, exercise, especially strength training, can help to build muscles that burn more calories, not to mention getting you that ripped figure. Yes, it was always good to dream that there was some magic pill in the market that could get you whipped in shape without any effort, but alas, it still remains a dream.

Strength training, done through weights at home or by hitting the gym is one of the surest ways that weight can be lost. Most of the time, it would be advisable to have a schedule for the days that you work out to concentrate on specific muscle groups. This targeted training helps to speed muscle development, leading to higher calorie usage and hence weight loss.

There will be loads of resources online on how to work out a proper strength training routine. The more important thing is to have the discipline to keep plugging at it until you see or feel the results. Believe me, it will be worth it.

Ketogenic Diet and Weight Loss

Having touched on what weight loss was and the common principles behind it, let us now look at how the ketogenic diet can become one of your staunchest allies in the battle of the bulge.

Being mindful of hunger – Like we said earlier, keeping hunger pangs at bay is one of the most important ways to ensure your weight loss regime is on track. The keto diet does this precisely by encouraging the consumption of fats, which by nature is more satiating and gives you the feeling of fulfilment and hence stops those frequent trips to the kitchen pantry for more food.

The other spiffy thing about going on the keto diet is the resultant leveling of your insulin levels. Insulin is known to induce the feeling of hunger and when ketosis kicks in, you no longer have those roller coaster ups and downs that is associated with the consumption of carbs and with that stability means your hunger pangs are held largely at bay due to the reduction of insulin produced by your body.

Now, you will eat when your body truly feels hunger and that is really quite liberating. Not to mention that because of this removal of hunger pangs from the overall equation, your weight loss journey will definitely become much, much simpler.

Quicker recovery from exercise – Whilst we engage in strength training in our bid to lose weight and get in shape, our bodies need time to recover from the physical activity. Practitioners of the keto diet will find that their recovery time will be somewhat quicker than others.

The reduction of carbohydrates to be replaced by fats is one of the main reasons why overall body inflammation levels will come down. Once inflammation is down, your muscles tend to recover faster from fatigue and this allows you to put in more sessions due to the shortened recovery period.

With the more stable energy levels achieved due to less fluctuations in the blood sugar levels, again due to the diet switch, this then allows you to work out without feeling faintish or light headed, typical symptoms of hypoglycemia or just simple lack of glucose in the bloodstream. Because you are burning fats and producing ketones as a more stable energy source!

More motivation from quicker results – Quick question, which would you prefer, a weight loss method that requires you to toil consistently at it for up to six months a pop and having a loss of four or five pounds to show for it, or the ketogenic diet that can see weight loss come in the range of twenty to thirty pounds within six to seven weeks?

If you are like me, then the choice would be the latter. Quicker results, especially in the arena of weight loss, is almost always going to be a welcome morale booster. When you literally see how much weight you have lost within those short weeks, it gives you that confidence that this method really works and you gain that conviction and strength to keep going.

What really happens here when you transit over to the keto diet is the fact that you have lowered insulin levels. Heightened insulin tells our kidneys to retain more salt and water, so when the insulin levels decrease, we have consequently lesser salt and water retention. This leads to a quick decrease in the number on the weighing scales, but more importantly, the keto diet also provides for a sustained drive in the loss of body weight through the burning of fat stores.

Some Tips for Weight Loss

This is by no means an exhaustive list but just something to let you kick start the weight loss journey if you haven't already. The tips are all quickly actionable and easy to follow, though some may require a little more effort than the other, these are all ideas which have been known to work for people in pursuit of weight loss.

Record what you eat – Get a note book if you are of the more pen and paper variety, or simply just use the note function in your smart phone to record down the food that you are consuming throughout the day. This gives you a sense of accountability when you sit down at the end of the day and review what you have eaten. You might be surprised at the amount of food you have taken in and this will serve as a timely reminder to do better the next day.

Get an accountability partner – Many people do better in tasks that require discipline when they are required to report to somebody else. Getting an accountability partner will give that added sense of responsibility as well as the desire not to disappoint the partner when you report on your weight loss daily activities. Having someone to cajole and encourage you during this period can be also immensely gratifying, and that could be the added push to keep you on track for the weight loss journey.

Get enough sleep – It is by no means a measure of surprise to know that lack of sleep hampers your weight loss efforts by the simple increase of the hormone cortisol in our body system. Cortisol increases our appetite and hunger sensations, which is why getting sufficient sleep can do simple wonders in letting you shed the excess pounds. You will feel less cranky and more energized too!

Be mindful when eating – We get the feeling of fullness and satiation when we actually concentrate on the food that we are chewing and not get distracted by the ever-present mobile devices or the other assorted distractions available in this modern world whilst we are having our meals. When eating, just eat! I know, it is easier said than done, but you can try counting the number of chews for that mouthful of food, get to seven or ten chews before swallowing. It helps to focus your mind back onto the food that you consume and as a bonus, you are helping your stomach with better digestion as well!

Avoid processed foods – Yeap, that means the ice-creams, donuts and creamy cakes have really got to take a backseat when it comes to your food selection. Pile on whole and natural foods because those are nutrient dense items that will ensure you do not take in empty calories. Most of the processed food found today contain quite a bit of sugar and are pretty deficient in the nutrients department, hence the term empty calories! The sugar eats into your calorie daily limit while not providing you with the essential nutrients your body needs. Go for chicken meat instead of chicken nuggets, whole potatoes instead of fries. You get the idea.

Chapter 5
Low Carb High Fat Recipes To Get You Started

This chapter gives you a few simple recipes for 4 meals a day: breakfast, lunch, a small snack, and dinner. This will give you the kick start on what to prepare for your meals on your ketogenic journey!

Breakfast Recipes

Currant Flaxseed Muffins

Nutritional value per muffin: Calories – 120 gm, Fat – 9.4 gm, Proteins – 4.2 gm, Carbs – 1.2 gm

Ingredients (makes 9 muffins)
- Ground flaxseed – 1 cup
- Red currants – ½ cup
- Erythritol – 1/3 cup
- Baking powder – ½ tbsp
- Cinnamon powder, ½ tbsp
- Eggs – 3
- Salt – ½ tsp
- Coconut oil – 3 tbsp
- Almond milk – 2 tbsp
- Vanilla extract – 1 tsp

Method: In a bowl, mix ground flaxseed with all the other dry ingredients. In a different bowl, mix all the wet ingredients. Now pour the wet mixture into the dry mixture and combine thoroughly. Fold in the red currants and mix again till the fruits are evenly spread in the muffin dough. Fill silicone muffin cups with the dough (3/4 full) and bake in a preheated oven at 350F for about 15 minutes. Once cooked, remove the muffins from the oven and allow them to cool; and dig in.

Breakfast Recipes

Oopsie Rolls

Nutritional value per roll: Calories – 45, Fat – 3.8gm, Protein – 2.3 gm, Carbs – 0

Ingredients (makes 12 rolls)
- Large eggs – 3
- Cream cheese – 3 oz
- Cream of tartar – 1/8 tsp
- Salt – 1/8 tsp

Method: Separate the eggs into white and yolks and keep in different bowls. With an electric mixer, beat the egg whites till bubbly. Now, add the cream of tartar and beat it till the formation of a stiff peak. In the yolk bowl, add the cream cheese and a little salt. Beat this mixture till you get a pale yellow color and the quantity has doubled in size. Now, fold in the egg white mixture gently. Onto a butter-lined cookie sheet, pour this folded mixture in small portion sizes and bake for 30-40 minutes in a preheated oven at 300F.

Breakfast Recipes

Keto Waffles

Nutritional Value per waffle: Calories – 280, Fat – 26 gm, Proteins – 7 gm, Carbs – 4.5 gm

Ingredients (Serves 5)
- Eggs – 5
- Coconut flour – 2 tbsp
- Artificial sweetener of your choice – 3-5 tbsp
- Baking powder – 1 tbsp
- Full-fat milk – 3 tbsp
- Melted butter – 4 oz

Method: Separate the yolks and egg whites. In one bowl, beat the whites till a stiff peak is formed. In another bowl, mix the coconut flour, egg yolks, baking powder, and stevia. To this, add the melted butter gradually and combine to get a smooth non-lumpy consistency. Add the vanilla extracts and milk and mix thoroughly. Gently fold in the beaten egg whites keeping as much of the air as possible. Pour this onto a warm waffle maker and cook until beautifully golden brown. Enjoy your breakfast.

Breakfast Recipes

Pumpkin Maple Flaxseed Muffins

Nutritional value per muffin: Calories – 120, Fat – 8.4 gm, Protein – 4.7 gm, Carbs – 2.2 gm

Ingredients (makes 10 muffins)
- Ground flaxseed – 1 ¼ cup
- Erythritol – 1/3 cup
- Baking powder – ½ tbsp
- Cinnamon – ½ tbsp
- Salt – ½ tsp
- Pumpkin puree – 1 cup
- Maple Syrup – ¼ cup
- Pumpkin pie spice – 1 tbsp
- Coconut oil – 2tbsp
- Egg – 1
- Apple cider vinegar – ½ tsp
- Vanilla extract – ½ tsp

Method: Mix all the dry ingredients and combine to form an even mixture. To this, add the pumpkin and mix thoroughly. Now, add vanilla extract, pumpkin spice, maple syrup, coconut oil, the egg, and the apple cider vinegar. Mix all the ingredients well. In silicone muffin molds, spoon out the dough to fill ¾th of the cups. You could top with some pumpkin seeds. Bake in a preheated oven at 350F for 20 minutes. Once cooked, remove the muffins and cool well before digging in.

Lunch Recipes

Bacon Burger without the bun

Nutritional value (for 4 portions): Calories – 890, Fat – 68 gm, Protein – 54.4 gm, Carbs – 8 gm

Ingredients (for 4 servings)
For almond butter sauce:
- Almond butter – 1 cup
- Water – 1 cup
- Peeled garlic cloves – 4
- Chili peppers – 4
- Coconut amino – 6 tbsp
- Artificial sweetener (AS)– 1 tsp
- Rice vinegar – 1 tbsp

For Burger:
- Grass-fed beef – 1.5 pounds
- Pepper Jack Cheese – 4 slices
- Uncured bacon – 8 slices
- Red onion – 1 large (cut into ¼-inch thick slices)
- Romaine lettuce – 8 large leaves
- Sea salt
- Black pepper

Method to make almond butter sauce: Mix water and almond butter in a saucepan and on a low flame, bring to a gentle simmer. Continue to stir and cook till you get a thick consistency. To this, add the coconut amino and mix. In a food processor, blend together the garlic, chili peppers, AS, and the vinegar to get a smooth paste. Add this paste to the almond butter and mix thoroughly.

Method to make the burgers: Shape the beef into 4 patties and cook them on a broiler pan along with a seasoning of salt and pepper. Broil till the patties are nicely golden brown on both sides (it should take about 5-7 minutes on each side). Now, remove them from the broiler pan; place the cheese slices over each and put them back into the broiler. Cook till the cheese melts.

On a skillet, fry and cook the bacon slices and drain them on a paper towel. Now you are ready to assemble the burger. Place two leaves of lettuce at the bottom; place the patties over them; place the red onion slice; add the almond butter sauce, and finally top with the bacon. Repeat for the other patties too.

Lunch Recipes

Fennel Walnut Chicken Salad

Nutritional Value (per serving): Calories – 200, Fat – 16 gm, Protein – 8 gm, Carbs – 3 gm

Ingredients (serves 6)
- Cooked and diced, skinless and boneless chicken breast – 3
- Coarsely chopped fresh fennel – 1 ½ cups
- Toasted and chopped walnuts – ¼ cup
- Mayonnaise – ¼ cup
- Walnut oil – 2 tbsp
- Lemon juice – 2 tbsp
- Chopped fennel fronds – 2 tbsp
- Pressed garlic cloves – 2
- Cayenne powder – 1/8 tsp
- Salt and pepper – to taste

Method: Toss together walnuts, fennel, and chicken in a large bowl. In a medium-sized bowl, whisk walnut oil, mayonnaise, fennel fronds, lemon juice, cayenne, and garlic till you get a smooth mixture. Pour this dressing over the chicken mixture and toss till all ingredients are coated well. Add salt and pepper to your taste. Chill the salad in the fridge for about an hour and enjoy your lunch.

Lunch Recipes

Sardine-Stuffed Avocado

Nutritional value (per serving): Calories – 633, Fat – 52.6 gm, Proteins – 27.2 gm, Carbs – 19.5 gm

Ingredients (one serving):
- Avocado – 1 large (seed removed and halved)
- Drained sardines – 1 tin
- Mayonnaise – 1 tbsp
- Spring onion – 1 bunch
- Lemon juice – 1 tbsp
- Turmeric powder – ¼ tsp
- Salt – ¼ tsp

Method: Place the drained sardines in a bowl. Scoop out the middle part of the avocado leaving out about 1 inch of the flesh from around the skin. To the sardines, add chopped spring onions, mayonnaise, and turmeric powder and mix well. Put in the scooped out part of the avocado flesh, pour in the lemon juice, and mix all the ingredients thoroughly. Add salt if necessary. Put this filling into each half of the scooped out avocado and enjoy your lunch.

Lunch Recipes

Garlic Lemon Shrimp Pasta

Nutritional value (per saving): Calories – 360, Fat – 21 gm, Protein – 36 gm, Carbs – 3.5 gm

Ingredients (for 4 servings):
- Gluten-free shirataki noodles – 2 packets
- Butter – 2 tbsp
- Olive oil – 2 tbsp
- Garlic – 4 cloves
- Lemon (sliced) – ½
- Raw shrimp (large) – 1 pound
- Paprika – ½ tsp
- Fresh basil
- Salt and pepper

Method: Cook the noodles as per the instructions given on the packet. Alternatively, you can follow these instructions. Drain the noodles and discard all the water. Do this through a cooking sieve and wash it under running water. Transfer into a pot with boiling water and cook for 2-3 minutes to remove the unpleasant odor. When the noodles are cooked, dry roast them on a pan till all the water has evaporated completely. This will help in greater absorption of flavors.

Heat olive oil and butter in a pan; put in crushed garlic and sauté till you smell the aroma of garlic. Add the sliced lemon and the shrimp. Cook each side of the shrimp for about 3 minutes. When the shrimps are opaque and cooked, add the noodles and season with paprika, salt and pepper. Toss everything together and mix thoroughly. Remove from heat and sprinkle some fresh basil over your delicious lunch before your dig in.

Snack Recipes

Lemon Raspberry Popsicle

Nutritional value (per Popsicle): Calories – 151, Fat – 16 gm, Proteins – 0.5 gm, Carbs – 2 gm

Ingredients (for 6 popsicles):
- Raspberries – 100 gm
- Lemon juice – from half a lemon
- Coconut oil – ¼ cup
- Coconut milk – 1 cup
- Sour cream – ¼ cup
- Heavy cream – ¼ cup
- Guar Gum – ½ tsp
- Liquid Stevia – 20 drops

Method: Put all the ingredients in a blender and blitz them together till the raspberries are all smoothly combined and you get a nice smooth mixture. Strain it and remove all the raspberry seeds. Pour the strained mixture into Popsicle molds and freeze for at least 2 hours. Your raspberry lemon popsicles are ready!

Snack Recipes

Orange Coconut Fat Bombs

Nutritional Value (per fat bomb): Calories – 176, Fats – 20 gm, Proteins – 0.8 gm, Carbs – 0.7 gm

Ingredients (makes 10 orange coconut fat bombs):
- Coconut Oil – ½ cup
- Heavy Whipping Cream – ½ cup
- Cream cheese – 4 oz
- Orange Vanilla Extract – 1 tsp
- Liquid Stevia – 10 drops

Method: Using an immersion blender, blitz all the ingredients together. If the ingredients are very hard, microwave for about 30 seconds to soften and then blend them together. Add the liquid stevia and the orange vanilla essence and mix thoroughly with a spoon. Spread the mixture onto silicone molds and freeze for about 2-3 hours. Once completely frozen, remove from the mold and enjoy your orange coconut fat bombs.

Snack Recipes

Neapolitan Fat Bombs

Nutritional value (of one fat bomb): Calories – 102, Fat – 10.9 gm, Proteins – 0.6 gm, Carbs – 0.4 gm

Ingredients (serves 24 fat bombs)
- Butter – ½ cup
- Coconut oil – ½ cup
- Sour cream – ½ cup
- Cream cheese – ½ cup
- Erythritol – 2 tbsp
- Liquid Stevia – 25 drops
- Cocoa powder – 2 tbsp
- Vanilla extract – 1 tsp
- Strawberries – 2 medium

Method: Combine coconut oil, butter, cream cheese, sour cream, liquid stevia and erythritol in a large mixing bowl. Use an immersion blender to blitz together all these ingredients to get a smooth mixture. Divide this mixture equally into 3 different smaller bowls. To one bowl, add strawberries; to the second bowl, add cocoa powder; to the third bowl, add vanilla extract.

Again mix the ingredients in each of the bowls using an immersion blender. Pour the chocolate-laced part into a container that has a spout. Pour this into fat bomb molds and freeze for about 30 minutes. Over this frozen layer, pour the vanilla mixture and freeze again for 30 minutes. Over this, pour the strawberry mixture and freeze for at least one hour for the last time. Once, the fat bombs are frozen well, remove from the molds and enjoy!

Snack Recipes

Peanut Butter Chocolate Fat Bomb

Nutritional value (per fat bomb): Calories – 208, Fats – 20 gm, Proteins – 4.4 gm, Carbs – 0.4 gm

Ingredients (to make 8 fat bombs):
- Coconut oil – ½ cup
- Cocoa powder – ¼ cup
- Peanut butter powder – 4 tbsp
- Hemp seeds (shelled) – 6 tbsp
- Heavy Cream – 2 tbsp
- Vanilla extract – 1 tsp
- Liquid stevia – 28 drops
- Unsweetened shredded coconut – ¼ cup

Method: Combine all the dry ingredients; add coconut oil and mix thoroughly so that you get a nice smooth paste. Add liquid stevia, heavy cream, and vanilla. Again, combine thoroughly till you get a nice creamy texture. Put the shredded coconut on a plate. Roll out balls with the mixture/dough and then coat them with the shredded coconut. Keep in the freezer for about 20 minutes to set well. Once frozen well, your fat bombs are ready to dig in!

Dinner recipes

Broccoli Soup

Nutritional value (per serving size of 130 gm): Calories – 272, Fats – 23 gm, Proteins – 10 gm, Carbs – 7 gm

Ingredients (serves 4)
- Heavy cream – ¼ cup
- Cream cheese – ¼ cup
- Sour cream – ¼ cup
- Almond milk – ¼ cup
- Cheddar cheese – 115 gm
- Broccoli – 200 gm
- Half a large onion
- Chicken Bouillon – ½ a cube

Method: Cut the broccoli into florets and steam them either in the microwave or on a stove (for about 3 minutes). Into a blender, add all the liquid ingredients and blitz together. Add the broccoli, cheese, and the onions too at this point and blend all together. Shred the bouillon cube and sprinkle over the soup. Pour into soup bowls or ramekins, sprinkle some cheddar cheese over the top, and serve.

Dinner recipes

Beef and Bacon Rolls

Nutritional Value (per serving consisting of 4 pieces): Calories – 215, Fats – 10 gm, Proteins – 29 gm, Carbs – 0 gm

Ingredients (serves 4):
- Beef – 16 oz
- Bacon – 4 slices
- Steak seasoning – as per your taste

Method: Preheat oil in your deep fryer to about 370F. Cut the beef into small bite-sized rectangular pieces of approximately 1-inch by 1-inch. Rub the pieces with steak seasoning. Wrap the pieces with bacon and stab these bacon-wrapped beef pieces onto a bent metal skewer. Now, deep-fry these succulent pieces of meat in your preheated fryer for 3 minutes. The bacon sticks on the beef beautifully during the frying process. Your beef and bacon rolls are ready.

Dinner recipes

Fried Radish Hash Browns

Nutritional value (per serving made up of 3 pancakes): Calories – 238, Fats – 18 gm, Proteins – 10 gm, Carbs – 10 gm

Ingredients (serves 3):
- Radishes – 1 lb.
- Shallots – 2
- Paprika – 1/4 tsp
- Thyme – ¼ tsp
- Salt – ¼ tsp
- Egg – 1 whole and 1 yolk
- Coconut flour – 1 tbsp
- Cheddar cheese – 2 oz
- Bacon Grease – 1 tbsp
- Butter – 1 tbsp

Method: Wash the radishes well and chop off the tops and the bottoms. Either by using a food processor or a simple manual grater shred the radishes into thin shavings. Peel and slice the shallots thinly. Mix all the ingredients (except the grease and butter) in a mixing bowl. In a skillet, heat the grease and the butter together. Take a bit of the radish mixture and make a rough pattie-shaped hash brown on the skillet. Avoid making a large size as flipping over will be a problem. Cook till both sides are brown and crispy.

Dinner recipes

Zucchini Noodles with Lamb Meatballs

Nutritional value (per serving): Calories – 426, Fats – 30 gm, Proteins – 23 gm, Carbs – 13 gm

Ingredients (serves 4):
- Zucchini – 2 lb.
- Pasta sauce (low carb) – 16 oz
- Ground lamb – 1 lb.
- Shallots (chopped) – 2
- The yolk of one egg
- Cinnamon powder – 1 tsp
- Cumin – 1 tsp
- Cayenne powder, red pepper flakes, salt and pepper – to taste

Method: Using either a veggie spiral slicer or julienne blades on a mandoline, make your zoodles (noodles of zucchini). Stop slicing with the seeds start to show. The skin part and the meat parts close to the skin are solid and good for zoodles.

Mix all the remaining ingredients together (except the pasta sauce) and make 16 meatballs of approximately 1 oz each. Place them on a foil-lined baking tray and bake the meatballs for 12 minutes in a preheated oven at 375F.

Now, take the pasta sauce in a pan and heat till it starts to bubble. To this, add the zoodles and continue cooking for another 3-4 minutes. Add the meatballs to this and gently mix everything together. Your zucchini noodle with meat sauce dinner is ready to be dug in.

Some Additional Tips for Improved Success From Your Keto Diets

Drink plenty of water – The reason I want to reiterate this point is because it is easier said than done. We get so caught up with our daily routines that we forget to drink ample water. Decide how much water is needed for you and fill up 3-4 small-sized bottles and keep them on your table. Make sure by the evening all the bottles are emptied. Some of you will be worried about the idea of drinking too much water, all hail the internet for the dispersal of such information! But trust me, it is far easier for you to find yourself getting by on lesser water than your body requires rather than the opposite. So drink up. Science has proven that an intake of about 1-2 liters of water every two hours is fairly optimal for the human system.

Practice Intermittent Fasting – Without going overboard, this is a great way to get into and to maintain ketosis. However, get into the habit of low-carb before you try this. You could try a cycle fasting method wherein for about 3 days a week, you fast for 16 hours by skipping either dinner or breakfast. Another way of intermittent fasting is to eat only 2 meals a day with 6-8 hour gap between them. This way you are reducing calories and forcing your body to burn more fats. One thing to note here is that if during the course of your ketogenic journey, you find yourself not feeling that hungry anyway even after only one meal a day, it has of course to be a large meal at that, then you are very well inadvertently practicing some form of fasting. This does not have to be a conscious idea that requires you to say that you are starting to fast. Just go with the flow sometimes and listen to what the body tells you. It knows best!

Improve bowel movement – constipation is one of the most important challenges faced by people on keto diets. Avoid it by enhancing intake of fermented foods such as kimchi and sauerkraut; try magnesium supplements, include ample fiber in your diet, and again drink plenty of water. Get in some coconut oil as well if your bowels aren't moving as much as they are supposed to. Take in small amounts, perhaps 1-2 teaspoons of coconut oil if you are not used to it at the start, then slowly increase it to 1 tablespoon in the morning and night if you prefer.

Make prudent carb choices – Low-carb is critical for the success of ketogenic diets. However, choose your carbs prudently. Avoid starchy veggies; instead choose nutrient-rich non-starchy vegetables like cucumber, zucchini, fresh green leaves including spinach and lettuce etc. This way your carbs are under check and your get ample fiber into your system too.

Now that you have an idea of the kind of recipes that you should work on, let me give you a 4-week meal plan to help you get started on your ketogenic diet. This next chapter deals with an easy-to-follow meal plan for 4 weeks.

Chapter 6
28 Days Pre-Planned

Planning is critical to the success of any venture, and so with ketogenic diets. This chapter is dedicated to giving you a simple 4-week meal plan. Such ready-made plans take off much of the struggle associated with getting started and maintaining a ketogenic lifestyle. However, this is definitely not a blanket plan that can fit everybody's needs, I do reckon that no such thing exists. What it can do for you is pretty much alleviate some of the thinking of what to eat for your meals whilst on the ketogenic diet. This meal plan is keeping a daily nutritional requirement of approximately 1400 to 1800 calories.

Week One

Day One

- Total calories – 1596

- Fat -132 gm

- Carbs – 14 gm

- Protein – 88 gm

- Breakfast – Three one-inch squares of sausage and spinach frittatas and coffee with 2 tbsp of heavy whipped cream
- Morning Snack – ½ an avocado with a light seasoning of salt and pepper
- Lunch – ½ cup of egg salad consisting of 1 boiled egg, 4 romaine lettuce leaves and 2 slices of cooked bacon
- Evening snack – 24 raw almonds

- Dinner – Rotisserie chicken – 6 oz, ¾ cup of cauliflower gratin, 2 cups of chopped romaine lettuce and 2 tbsp of sugar-free salad dressing
- Dessert – 3 strawberries

Day Two

- Total calories – 1560

- Fat -126 gm

- Carbs – 18.5 gm

- Protein – 88 gm

- Breakfast – 3 scrambled or fried eggs, 1 tsp butter, 2 pieces of cooked bacon and coffce with 2 tbsp of heavy whipped cream
- Morning snack – 5 celery sticks with 2 tbsp of almond butter
- Lunch – 2 cups of chopped romaine lettuce, 1 cup of rotisserie chicken and 2 tbsp of sugar-free salad dressing
- Evening snack – ½ an avocado with a little salt and pepper
- Dinner – 1 cooked and sliced Italian sausage link, 1 cup of cooked broccoli, 1 tbsp butter, and 2 tbsp grated parmesan cheese
- Dessert – 2 squares of 90% chocolate

Day Three

- Total calories – 1567

- Fat -119 gm

- Carbs – 18 gm

- Protein – 78 gm

- Breakfast – 2 cream cheese pancakes, 2 pieces of cooked bacon and coffee with 2 tbsp heavy whipped cream
- Morning snack – 2 string cheese
- Lunch – 1 cooked and sliced Italian sausage link and 1 cup of cauliflower gratin
- Evening snack – 1 cup of bone soup
- Dinner – 1 ½ cup of chili spaghetti squash casserole, 2 cups of raw baby spinach and 1 tbsp of sugar-free salad dressing
- Dessert – 100ml coconut water

Day Four

- Total calories – 1362

- Fat -112 gm

- Carbs – 19.5 gm

- Protein – 69 gm

- Breakfast – 1 jalapeno muffin with cheddar cheese, 2 scrambled eggs (with 1 tsp butter), 1 pieces of cooked bacon, and coffee with 2 tbsp of heavy whipped cream
- Morning snack – ½ an avocado with a sprinkling of salt and pepper
- Lunch – 1 ½ cup chili spaghetti squash casserole
- Evening snack – 1 cup of bone broth
- Dinner – ½ cup of salad made with raw cauliflower, artichokes, radish, and some Italian seasoning, 4 feta and sundried tomato meatballs, 2 cups of raw baby spinach, and 1 tbsp of sugar-free salad dressing

- Dessert – 10 raw walnuts

Day Five

- Total calories – 1586

- Fat -132 gm

- Carbs – 18.5 gm

- Protein – 81 gm

- Breakfast – Three one-inch squares of sausage and spinach frittatas and coffee with 2 tbsp of heavy whipped cream
- Morning snack – 1 cup of bone broth
- Lunch – ½ cup of egg salad consisting of 1 boiled egg, 4 romaine lettuce leaves and 2 slices of cooked bacon
- Evening snack – 5 sticks of celery with 2 tbsp of almond butter
- Dinner – 1 cup of Cuban Pot Roast, 2 cups of romaine lettuce, 2 tbsp sour cream, 1 chopped cilantro, and ¼ cup of shredded cheddar cheese
- Dessert – 1 small packet of salted seaweed

Day Six

- Total calories – 1532

- Fat -122 gm

- Carbs – 19.5 gm

- Protein – 89 gm

- Breakfast – 3 scrambled or fried eggs, 1 tsp butter, 2 pieces of cooked bacon and coffee with 2 tbsp of heavy whipped cream
- Morning snack – 24 raw almonds
- Lunch – 2 cups of chopped romaine lettuce, 1 cup of rotisserie chicken and 2 tbsp of sugar-free salad dressing
- Evening snack – 1 cup of bone broth
- Dinner – ½ cup of salad made with raw cauliflower, artichokes, radish, and some Italian seasoning, 4 feta and sundried tomato meatballs, 2 cups of raw baby spinach, and 1 tbsp of sugar-free salad dressing
- Dessert – 100ml of coconut water

Day Seven

- Total calories – 1584

- Fat -128 gm

- Carbs – 18 gm

- Protein – 90 gm

- Breakfast – Three one-inch squares of sausage and spinach frittatas and coffee with 2 tbsp of heavy whipped cream
- Morning snack – 2 string cheese
- Lunch – 1 cooked and sliced Italian sausage link, 1 cup of cooked broccoli, 1 tbsp butter, and 2 tbsp grated parmesan cheese
- Evening snack – 1 cup of bone broth
- Dinner – 1 cup of Cuban Pot Roast, 2 cups of chopped romaine lettuce, 2 tbsp of sour cream, and ¼ cup shredded cheddar cheese
- Dessert – 10 walnuts

Week Two

Day One

- Total calories – 1456

- Fat - 122 gm

- Carbs – 17.5 gm

- Protein – 72 gm

- Breakfast – 2 Cream Cheese pancakes, 2 pieces of cooked bacon, and coffee with 2 tbsp heavy whipped cream
- Morning snack – 12 raw almonds
- Lunch – 1 cup jalapeno soup and 1 jalapeno muffin with cheddar cheese
- Evening snack – 1 cup bone soup
- Dinner – ¼ flaxseed pizza made with flaxseeds and parmesan cheese, 2 cups of raw baby spinach and 1 tbsp of sugar-free salad dressing
- Dessert – 3 strawberries

Day Two

- Total calories – 1520

- Fat - 122 gm

- Carbs – 16.5 gm

- Protein – 89 gm

- Breakfast – 2 scrambled eggs made with 1 tsp of butter, 2 pieces of cooked bacon, and coffee with 2 tbsp of heavy whipped cream

- Morning Snack – ½ an avocado
- Lunch – ¼ flax pizza
- Evening snack – 1 cup of bone soup
- Dinner – 1 paprika chicken thigh, ½ cup of cauliflower gratin, 1 cups of raw baby spinach, and 1 tbsp of sugar-free salad dressing
- Dessert – 10 walnuts

Day Three

- Total calories – 1800

- Fat - 154 gm

- Carbs – 17.5 gm

- Protein – 86 gm

- Breakfast – Three one-inch squares of sausage and spinach frittatas and coffee with 2 tbsp of heavy whipped cream
- Morning snack – ½ an avocado
- Lunch – 1 paprika chicken thigh and ½ cup of cheesy cauliflower puree
- Evening snack – 12 raw almonds
- Dinner – 1 cup jalapeno soup, 1 jalapeno muffin with cheddar cheese, 2 cups of chopped romaine lettuce and 2 tbsp of sugar-free salad dressing
- Dessert – 100ml coconut water

Day Four

- Total calories – 1669

- Fat - 141 gm

- Carbs – 18 gm

- Protein – 82 gm

- Breakfast – 1 jalapeno muffin with cheddar cheese, 2 scrambled eggs (with 1 tsp butter), 1 pieces of cooked bacon, and coffee with 2 tbsp of heavy whipped cream
- Morning snack – 1 cup of bone soup
- Lunch – ¼ flax meal pizza
- Evening snack – ½ an avocado
- Dinner – 1 cup of jalapeno soup, 1 jalapeno muffin with cheddar cheese, 2 cups of romaine lettuce, and 2 tbsp of sugar-free salad dressing
- Dessert – 2 squares of 90% chocolate

Day Five

- Total calories – 1382

- Fat - 106 gm

- Carbs – 18 gm

- Protein – 89 gm

- Breakfast – 2 cream cheese pancakes, 2 pieces of cooked bacon, and coffee with 2 tbsp of heavy whipped cream
- Morning Snack - 1 jalapeno muffin with cheddar cheese
- Lunch – ¼ flax meal pizza, 2 cups of raw baby spinach, and 1 tbsp sugar-free salad dressing
- Evening snack – 1 cup of bone soup
- Dinner – 3 meatballs with parmesan, 2 cups of romaine lettuce, and 2 tbsp of sugar-free salad dressing
- Dessert – 1 small packet of salted seaweed

Day Six

- Total calories – 1843

- Fat - 153 gm

- Carbs – 16.5 gm

- Protein – 100 gm

- Breakfast – 2 scrambled eggs made with 1 tsp of butter, 2 pieces of cooked bacon, and coffee with 2 tbsp of heavy whipped cream
- Morning snack – 12 raw almonds
- Lunch – 1 cup jalapeno soup and 1 jalapeno muffin with cheddar cheese
- Evening snack – 1 cup of bone soup
- Dinner – 1 paprika chicken thigh, ½ cheesy cauliflower puree, 2 cups of chopped romaine lettuce, and 2 tbsp of sugar-free salad dressing
- Dessert – 3 strawberries

Day Seven

- Total calories – 1518

- Fat - 118 gm

- Carbs – 19 gm

- Protein – 95 gm

- Breakfast – Three one-inch squares of sausage and spinach frittatas and coffee with 2 tbsp of heavy whipped cream
- Morning snack – 1 cup of bone soup
- Lunch – 3 meats with parmesan cheese

- Evening snack – ½ an avocado
- Dinner – 1 paprika chicken thigh, ½ cup of cheesy cauliflower puree, 2 cups of chopped romaine lettuce, 2 tbsp of sugar-free salad dressing
- Dessert – 2 squares of 90% chocolate

Week Three

Day One

- Total calories – 1518

- Fat - 118 gm

- Carbs – 19 gm

- Protein – 95 gm

- Breakfast – Two cream cheese pancakes, 2 pieces of cooked bacon, and coffee with 2 tbsp of heavy whipped cream
- Morning snack – 1 cup of bone soup
- Lunch – 3 meats with parmesan cheese
- Evening snack – ½ an avocado
- Dinner – 1 paprika chicken thigh, ½ cup of cheesy cauliflower puree, 2 cups of chopped romaine lettuce, 2 tbsp of sugar-free salad dressing
- Dessert – 1 small packet of salted seaweed

Day Two

- Total calories – 1843

- Fat - 153 gm

- Carbs – 16.5 gm

- Protein – 100 gm

- Breakfast – 1 jalapeno muffin with cheddar cheese, 2 scrambled eggs (with 1 spoon butter), 2 pieces of cooked bacon, and coffee with 2 tbsp of heavy whipped cream
- Morning snack – 12 raw almonds
- Lunch – 1 cup jalapeno soup and 1 jalapeno muffin with cheddar cheese
- Evening snack – 1 cup of bone soup
- Dinner – 1 paprika chicken thigh, ½ cheesy cauliflower puree, 2 cups of chopped romaine lettuce, and 2 tbsp of sugar-free salad dressing
- Dessert – 3 strawberries

Day Three

- Total calories – 1382

- Fat - 106 gm

- Carbs – 18 gm

- Protein – 89 gm

- Breakfast – 2 scrambled eggs made with 1 tsp of butter, 2 pieces of cooked bacon, and coffee with 2 tbsp of heavy whipped cream
- Morning Snack - 1 jalapeno muffin with cheddar cheese
- Lunch – ¼ flax meal pizza, 2 cups of raw baby spinach, and 1 tbsp sugar-free salad dressing
- Evening snack – 1 cup of bone soup
- Dinner – 3 meatballs with parmesano, 2 cups of romaine lettuce, and 2 tbsp of sugar-free salad dressing
- Dessert – 2 squares of 90% chocolate

Day Four

- Total calories – 1800

- Fat - 154 gm

- Carbs – 17.5 gm

- Protein – 86 gm

- Breakfast – 2 Cream cheese pancakes, 2 pieces of cooked bacon and coffee with 2 tbsp heavy whipped cream
- Morning snack – ½ an avocado
- Lunch – 1 paprika chicken thigh and ½ cup of cheesy cauliflower puree
- Evening snack – 12 raw almonds
- Dinner – 1 cup jalapeno soup, 1 jalapeno muffin with cheddar cheese, 2 cups of chopped romaine lettuce and 2 tbsp of sugar-free salad dressing
- Dessert – 1 small packet of salted seaweed

Day Five

- Total calories – 1520

- Fat - 122 gm

- Carbs – 16.5 gm

- Protein – 89 gm

- Breakfast – Three one-inch squares of sausage and spinach frittatas and coffee with 2 tbsp of heavy whipped cream
- Morning Snack – ½ an avocado
- Lunch – ¼ flax pizza

- Evening snack – 1 cup of bone soup
- Dinner – 1 paprika chicken thigh, ½ cup of cauliflower gratin, 1 cups of raw baby spinach, and 1 tbsp of sugar-free salad dressing
- Dessert – 10 walnuts

Day Six

- Total calories – 1596

- Fat - 132 gm

- Carbs – 14 gm

- Protein – 88 gm

- Breakfast – 2 scrambled eggs made with 1 tsp of butter, 2 pieces of cooked bacon, and coffee with 2 tbsp of heavy whipped cream
- Morning Snack – ½ an avocado with a light seasoning of salt and pepper
- Lunch – ½ cup of egg salad consisting of 1 boiled egg, 4 romaine lettuce leaves and 2 slices of cooked bacon
- Evening snack – 24 raw almonds
- Dinner – Rotisserie chicken – 6 oz, ¾ cup of cauliflower gratin, 2 cups of chopped romaine lettuce and 2 tbsp of sugar-free salad dressing
- Dessert – 2 squares of 90% chocolate

Day Seven

- Total calories – 1669

- Fat - 141 gm

- Carbs – 18 gm

- Protein – 82 gm

- Breakfast – 1 jalapeno muffin with cheddar cheese, 2 scrambled eggs (with 1 tsp butter), 1 pieces of cooked bacon, and coffee with 2 tbsp of heavy whipped cream
- Morning snack – 1 cup of bone soup
- Lunch – ¼ flax meal pizza
- Evening snack – ½ an avocado
- Dinner – 1 cup of jalapeno soup, 1 jalapeno muffin with cheddar cheese, 2 cups of romaine lettuce, and 2 tbsp of sugar-free salad dressing
- Dessert – 3 strawberries

Week Four

Day One

- Total calories – 1560

- Fat - 126 gm

- Carbs – 18.5 gm

- Protein – 88 gm

- Breakfast – 2 Cream cheese pancakes, 2 pieces of cooked bacon and coffee with 2 tbsp heavy whipped cream
- Morning snack – 5 celery sticks with 2 tbsp of almond butter
- Lunch – 2 cups of chopped romaine lettuce, 1 cup of leftover rotisserie chicken and 2 tbsp of sugar-free salad dressing
- Evening snack – ½ an avocado with a little salt and pepper

- Dinner – 1 cooked and sliced Italian sausage link, 1 cup of cooked broccoli, 1 tbsp butter, and 2 tbsp grated parmesan cheese
- Dessert – 100ml coconut water

Day Two

- Total calories – 1596

- Fat - 132 gm

- Carbs – 14 gm

- Protein – 88 gm

- Breakfast – Three one-inch squares of sausage and spinach frittatas and coffee with 2 tbsp of heavy whipped cream
- Morning Snack – ½ an avocado with a light seasoning of salt and pepper
- Lunch – ½ cup of egg salad consisting of 1 boiled egg, 4 romaine lettuce leaves and 2 slices of cooked bacon
- Evening snack – 24 raw almonds
- Dinner – Rotisserie chicken – 6 oz, ¾ cup of cauliflower gratin, 2 cups of chopped romaine lettuce and 2 tbsp of sugar-free salad dressing
- Dessert – 2 squares of 90% chocolate

Day Three

- Total calories – 1362

- Fat - 112 gm

- Carbs – 19.5 gm

- Protein – 69 gm

- Breakfast – 2 scrambled eggs made with 1 tsp of butter, 2 pieces of cooked bacon, and coffee with 2 tbsp of heavy whipped cream
- Morning Snack – ½ an avocado with a sprinkling of salt and pepper
- Lunch – 1 ½ cup chili spaghetti squash casserole
- Evening snack – 1 cup of bone broth
- Dinner – ½ cup of salad made with raw cauliflower, artichokes, radish, and some Italian seasoning, 4 feta and sundried tomato meatballs, 2 cups of raw baby spinach, and 1 tbsp of sugar-free salad dressing
- Dessert – 10 walnuts

Day Four

- Total calories – 1455

- Fat - 119 gm

- Carbs – 18 gm

- Protein – 78 gm

- Breakfast – 1 jalapeno muffin with cheddar cheese, 2 scrambled eggs (with 1 tsp butter), 1 pieces of cooked bacon, and coffee with 2 tbsp of heavy whipped cream
- Morning snack – 2 string cheese
- Lunch – 1 cooked and sliced Italian sausage link and 1 cup of cauliflower gratin
- Evening snack – 1 cup of bone soup
- Dinner – 1 ½ cup of chili spaghetti squash casserole, 2 cups of raw baby spinach and 1 tbsp of sugar-free salad dressing
- Dessert – 100ml coconut water

Day Five

- Total calories – 1584

- Fat - 128 gm

- Carbs – 18 gm

- Protein – 90 gm

- Breakfast – 2 cream cheese pancakes, 2 pieces of cooked bacon, and coffee with 2 tbsp of heavy whipped cream
- Morning snack – 2 string cheese
- Lunch – ½ cup of egg salad consisting of 1 boiled egg, 4 romaine lettuce leaves and 2 slices of cooked bacon
- Evening snack – 1 cup of bone broth
- Dinner – 1 cup of Cuban Pot Roast, 2 cups of chopped romaine lettuce, 2 tbsp of sour cream, and ¼ cup shredded cheddar cheese
- Dessert – 3 strawberries

Day Six

- Total calories – 1586

- Fat - 132 gm

- Carbs – 18.5 gm

- Protein – 81 gm

- Breakfast – Three one-inch squares of sausage and spinach frittatas and coffee with 2 tbsp of heavy whipped cream
- Morning snack – 1 cup of bone broth

- Lunch – 1 cooked and sliced Italian sausage link and 1 cup of cauliflower gratin
- Evening snack – 5 sticks of celery with 2 tbsp of almond butter
- Dinner – 1 cup of Cuban Pot Roast, 2 cups of romaine lettuce, 2 tbsp sour cream, 1 chopped cilantro, and ¼ cup of shredded cheddar cheese
- Dessert – 1 small packet of salted seaweed

Day Seven

- Total calories – 1532

- Fat - 122 gm

- Carbs – 19.5 gm

- Protein – 89 gm

- Breakfast – 3 scrambled or fried eggs, 1 tsp butter, 2 pieces of cooked bacon and coffee with 2 tbsp of heavy whipped cream
- Morning Snack – 24 raw almonds
- Lunch – 1 cup of Cuban Pot Roast, 2 cups of romaine lettuce, 2 tbsp sour cream, 1 chopped cilantro, and ¼ cup of shredded cheddar cheese
- Evening snack – 1 cup of bone broth
- Dinner – ½ cup of salad made with raw cauliflower, artichokes, radish, and some Italian seasoning, 4 feta and sundried tomato meatballs, 2 cups of raw baby spinach, and 1 tbsp of sugar-free salad dressing
- Dessert – 2 squares of 90% chocolate

If you notice, the above meal plan has many repeats. This is to enhance the ease of getting started. Do more of the same meals every so often and you will brush up your familiarity with it. Make meals for a week or a couple of days and store them in the fridge. You can then mix and match as per your convenience.

Another thing to note is that there is no harm repeating meals if you really find that you like one particular one. Of course, as humans our thirst for variety will invariably lead us to try new things, all the more so for food. That is why it must be stressed that this 28 day plan is essentially just a guide, it is something which can get you started, and for you to fall back on if you do run out of ideas.

Moreover, the recipes in the previous chapter have deliberately been left out here so that you get more options to try out your own meal plans. Perhaps, for the first two weeks, follow what I have given you in this chapter and then, when you have gained sufficient confidence in yourself, you will be able to create your own customized meal plans that are more in sync with your likes and dislikes. Feel free to innovate and try new things. You just have to remember to get your macros right and, again, drink sufficient water. Spices, except sugar and MSG, make your food tasty, delicious and fun. Experiment with them.

Conclusion
My Experience and What You Want To Know

When I first started out on the ketogenic diet, it was done so out of a feeling of hopelessness and despair, and perhaps throw in a bit of desperation as well. Alright, that sounded a trifle dramatic, but the truth was probably not too far off the mark either.

I had tried practically the stuff that was mentioned in the introduction of this book, the exercise machines, the different pills that were touted to be able to burn fat and lose weight, the different diets that gave me some results but then allowed the lost weight to come back on again with a vengeance after I couldn't stand the constant hunger that came with dieting.

So in effect, I was of the mindset that there was pretty much nothing to lose when I decided to go ahead with trying out this keto diet, and with this try, it effectively became part of my lifestyle for the past ten years and counting. I could still remember the time when I got on the bandwagon and it was practically a complete plunge into the deep for me. I made the decision to go on the diet and wham! I cut the carbs out from my diet that very day.

Now, there is really no right or wrong with this approach. Some people prefer easing themselves slowly into the diet, which means slowly reducing the carbs intake on a daily basis. Others, like myself, are, shall we say, a bit more anxious for results, and perhaps just a bit lazier in keeping track of the carb count, and hence take the route of cutting it drastically on the very first day of the diet.

I got on with it and more importantly kept up with the diet and its requirements. The first bout of side effects came pretty much within a few days of the start of the diet. One of the main things that really got into me was the lightheadedness that accompanied the transition of the body burning carbs to fats. I felt fatigued and it wasn't a pleasant experience. The cramps followed soon after, as I continued on during the early days. At that point in time, I did not have too much literature that is fairly available now, off or online, but I understood that these were side effects of having a body system that is changing the fuel it was burning for energy.

The keto-flu effects persisted for about a week, and this is for real, I started dropping pounds! I did the diet for a week and I was already seeing the results in terms of losing weight! I shed about 30 pounds within two weeks of starting the diet. The side effects, as promised, wore off as the body readjusted itself to burning fats. More importantly, was the physical feeling of having more energy as I went about my business day. I felt trimmer and the effect of the lost weight could really be seen on my physical frame. Having cut my waist line by one and half inches, I had to alter most of my pants and belt holes while I was at it in order to have a proper fit for my clothes.

Most of my friends and people around me started questioning me on what was going on, with some even heaping on the concern as they thought the weight loss was due to me being sick! When I told them about the ketogenic diet, and it being the cause of the serious, rapid weight loss, they were floored. And the detractors started to state their case. To be fair, some of them were genuinely concerned for me when I told them that I was consuming fats for meals. The usual statement about too much fats clogs your arteries and the standard mish mash on cardiovascular diseases. I thanked them for their concern and took time to educate those who were willing to listen, on what the ketogenic diet was really about. As time progressed, and I did not drop dead from a heart attack or suffer a stroke, whilst my lost weight stayed lost, and my health and physique improved in a large part due to the diet (as well as regular gym sessions), these well-meaning detractors started to get really interested in what I was doing. Not the ask and forget kind of interest, but interest that meant they were also keen to embark on the same ketogenic journey that I was also on. Naturally they began seeking me out for questions, and I have documented some of the more prominent ones below.

Is ketosis natural for humans – Bam! This is the big one to start off with and I must say, one of the more common ones to be asked together with whether ketosis was actually harmful or helpful to us. Usually I pretty much look them in the eye and readily tell them, if ketosis was not natural for human beings, then humans would probably have died off the planet eons ago.

The thing about ketosis is that it enables our body to survive and even thrive on ketones, which is an alternative fuel source to glucose. In the early days of men, when the land most definitely wasn't farmed and crops weren't grown, the common source of food was animal meat and consequently its fats. Early men definitely were in ketosis most of the time due to the high fat diet they consumed and it surely turned out well for them, considering we as humans became the dominant species on earth.

Why do we count carbs and not net carbs – A more technical question, and something which many turn to ask when they launch themselves into the ketogenic diet and then realize that they were not producing sufficient ketones to get the optimal effects.

Carbs are carbs, and the idea to count net carbs, discounting the fiber in the food, may very well be one of the key reasons why ketosis still proves to be elusive. When we set a carb limit for say 30 grams a day, we stick to that. Though some proponents of the net carb theory state that they do not consider fiber as carbs, I choose to err on the side of caution. After all, the ketogenic diet is espousing low carb and high fat consumption, hence I will do well to ensure that my daily carb intake remains low in order for me to remain in nutritional ketosis.

Remember, we always keep our carb intake low and then gradually work upwards to see what your own carbohydrate tolerance is.

Would I want to cycle in and out of ketosis – Some folks who tried the diet for a couple of months and were seeing good results from the diet decided to pose this question to me. They essentially wanted to bump up their carb intake again which would shake them out of ketosis for a variety of reasons. Some of them wanted to indulge themselves a little, after all, a low carb diet does not really allow for many of the sweet and decadent desserts that are so prevalent these days. Others thought that it would be good to have occasional bouts of carbohydrate consumption.

For me, my primary guiding light would be to always listen to your body and adjust your diet and lifestyle accordingly.

For the folks who generally want to have a cheat week or two after being on the ketogenic diet for two to three months, it is really up to them. I've only got to say that when the time comes for re-embarking on the diet, the side effects of getting started will hit once again, so you will have to grind through that particular period.

I did that a few times, getting out of ketosis, and then re-starting once again. Each time it would take me about a week to shake off the side effects and get my system running properly. One special note on this, whilst you are temporarily out of the diet, do not lose count of the carbs you consume daily. Think of it as a habit as it will help greatly when you restart the keto diet.

How long do I need to wait to see improvement in weight and health – This is a really personal question. I mean it! It depends on each person's body condition and also how soon can the system enter into an optimal ketone producing state.

Generally speaking, most people start to see results in terms of shedding weight within two to three weeks of going into ketosis. However, I have also known some friends who were on the diet for a month, and did not show much weight loss. This warranted some investigation and it was later found that this group of friends who seemed to not be reaping the benefits of the diet were actually doing some things wrong. Some were taking in way too much carbs, while others were not getting enough fats, hence they constantly felt hungry and that led to cheating whilst on the diet.

Eventually, we managed to straighten these issues out and I am happy to report that they saw good results when their body systems entered into nutritional ketosis. The key message that I want to get across is that the keto diet works, when it doesn't, it would be good to quickly examine the basics before condemning it to the tried and failed basket. Are you on a low carb, moderate protein and high fat diet? Are you counting your carbs such that you do not exceed your daily threshold? Are you getting enough healthy fats in your system for this diet to work? All these questions would be good to ask yourself should you find yourself not enjoying the benefits that the keto diet brings. Address them and if it still does not yield any results, then consider moving on to other options.

How do I get into ketosis if I am vegetarian – To be really honest, when I first got this question from one of my buddies, I was like, the keto diet is high fat, you probably will need to tuck into the fatty cuts of meat to make it work. However, I am glad to say that after some thinking and research, getting into ketosis is still possible while being a vegetarian.

For starters, you have got a major source of fat in terms of oils as well as butter. Again always get grass fed butter. Get your salad fix doused with olive oil and add in many pads of butter to get a highly satiating meal. Throw in some walnuts or macadamia nuts which have high fat content as well as not forgetting nature's fatty fruit the avocado, and your fat intake will likely be sufficient to get your system into ketosis.

The tricky part here will be managing the amount of vegetables that you consume, seeing as such that all the greens are considered carbs. Some of my friends get around it by going on a fat buffet. Drizzling olive oil on 40 grams of butter and just shoving it straight into their palate.

I for one most definitely do not recommend that. A more palatable way to get around this is really to make use of the avocado fruit in many of the meals, given its high fat to carb ratio. Granted, meal options are going to be more restricted than if you were eating meat, but this is one of the ways you can make the keto diet work while going vegetarian.

How long before the side effects of the keto diet wear off – Another favorite question that worked its way into the finals. I think it is probably the fact that we humans generally do not like to suffer, which is why we tend to seek knowledge on the potential sufferings that we are about to go through in order to make it more bearable.

While I would like to definitively give an answer on this, it really differs from person to person. Some I know get their systems straightened out within three days, while others need upward of a week and a half to ride out the side effects. Instead of focusing on how long the side effects last, I would rather zoom in on what we can do to make these side effects more pleasant.

Drinking more water, getting sufficient micronutrients through salt and electrolyte rich coconut water as well as brewing of bone broths are the common steps which I take whenever I need to combat these irksome side effects. That, and also a healthy dose of determination and commitment.

A Final Note

Whoosh! We have arrived at this juncture and I am so glad that you have chosen to take the steps out forward on this ketogenic journey. This book and its contents, I hope, have been able to give you a structured and actionable step by step plan to start the diet.

More importantly, it is my hope as well that the book has also given you the confidence booster and built up the commitment to stay on the diet. The benefits of ketosis awaits, and if health is wealth, you should be getting wealthy pretty soon!

There will be other books coming out on the ketogenic diet from me, so do look out for them. In the meantime, if you had enjoyed this book, please do leave a review for me on Amazon and I would be most grateful!

Thank you, stay healthy and happy!

About The Author.

Jamie Moore has always been fascinated by food and what it can do for the human body since young, so much so that he ended up putting on so much weight that the doctors' advice at one point was for him to be wheel chair bound because any physical activity was deemed too strenuous for him. Yes, even walking! Things came to a head after one particularly bad hospital episode and that triggered the process to finally shed the unwanted pounds.

It wasn't an easy road. Despite going on varying diets, weight loss regimes and spending on the latest exercise gear, the results just weren't manifesting itself. It wasn't until Jamie chanced upon the ketogenic diet that things got turned around for the better. Enthralled with what he had found and his own positive experiences with the diet for weight loss, Jamie took up distance learning courses to get accreditation on dieting and nutrition in order to further understand more about the ketogenic diet.

That was ten years ago. These days, Jamie does forty laps in the pool with regular gym sessions thrown in for good measure. He does not term himself as a health geek, but most of his friends beg to differ! They come to him for anything on diet, nutrition and exercise. That was also part of the reason why Jamie took to penning down what he knew into books which he hopes would be of help to people.